PRAISE FOR *THE ART OF ENGAGEMENT*

"Today at Panda Express, we're using the insights in *The Art of Engagement* to redesign every element of our restaurant training system. We're eliminating the manuals and PowerPoint presentations. Everything is being built around visual images that stimulate dialogue and drive action."

—*Tom Davin, CEO, Panda Restaurant Group, Inc.*

"The Strategic Engagement Process pioneered by Root Learning has proved invaluable in ensuring that our executives, managers, and frontline employees all know and understand how their efforts directly connect with our strategic plan."

—*Rich Meelia, President and CEO, Covidien*

"This book represents a career full of learning that Jim and his colleagues have acquired through years of helping organizations link 'Boardroom' strategy to front-line execution. Jim's 'story telling' provides a practical way to simplify complex concepts into workable solutions for your own organization."

—*Connie Colao, Chief People Officer, Taco Bell*

"Dialogue is the oxygen of change. The principles in *The Art of Engagement* have been vital in assisting Textron to change our conversations—which ultimately changed our results."

—*Lewis Campbell, CEO, Textron*

"The ideas Haudan describes in this book helped us find new and compelling ways to engage every single employee at Harley-Davidson in our critical business issues. These insights were an important contributor to the Partnership Philosophy . . . a philosophy that was pivotal to our success."

—*Rich Teerlink, Former Chairman and CEO, Harley-Davidson*

"Jim Haudan and his team at Root Learning have been instrumental partners in helping our brand grow through franchisee and team member engagement. They worked in partnership with our brand to design tools that stimulate conversation and help people come to their own conclusions about the direction of the brand. This led our franchisee and hotel teams to a feeling of ownership through authorship, versus mandated compliance. The use of Socratic dialogue to facilitate learning provides the road map that allows us to work together toward a common vision."

—*Gina Valenti, Senior Director—Brand Program Development & Integration, Hampton Brand Management, Hilton Hotels Corporation*

THE ART
of
ENGAGEMENT

Bridging the Gap
between People
and Possibilities

JIM HAUDAN
CEO, Root Learning

New York Chicago San Francisco Lisbon London
Madrid Mexico Milan New Delhi
San Juan Seoul Singapore Sydney Toronto

The McGraw·Hill Companies

7 8 9 0   DOC/DOC   1 4 3 2 1

ISBN   978-0-07-154485-6
MHID   0-07-154485-2

McGraw-Hill books are available at special quantity discounts to use as premiums and sales promotions, or for use in corporate training programs. To contact a representative, please visit the Contact Us pages at www.mhprofessional.com.

This book is printed on acid-free paper.

Michelle, Brad, Brooke, and Blake

To my wonderful wife and best friend for life . . .

Michelle, your belief in me and your unconditional love is my personal motivation to search for "better ways." You raise my understanding of compassion and caring to new heights every day.

To my daughter Brooke, and sons Brad and Blake. . .

Brooke, I will never forget your monumental advice, simple and to the point: "Whatever you do, don't do it for the money." Your wisdom on the things that really matter is a guiding light.

Brad, your pursuit of excellence, search for innovation, and your hunger to learn are a constant inspiration.

Blake, thank you for being the model for taking on obstacles with a can-do attitude and for standing so confidently in your own skin.

Love is the ultimate engagement. Thank you for yours. You can count on mine. It makes it all worthwhile.

To the people of Root Learning. . .

The Art of Engagement is not the work of one person. It embodies the passion, talent, dreams, hard work, and pioneering spirit of hundreds of people, past and present, who contribute the best of themselves every day at Root Learning. For them, every engagement—with each other or with clients—is an adventure to help others discover the incredible capability that lies within a person, a team, or an organization . . . always with the belief that people have much more power than they ever thought to change the world around them.

CONTENTS

Part 4: The Process of Strategic Engagement   165

ACKNOWLEDGMENTS

For 13 years, I had the privilege of working with Root Learning's founding partner, Randy Root. Randy worked to knit together analytical insight, critical thinking, and creativity to launch a movement. In his words, this movement was about "democratizing strategic information." He believed that people at all levels of any organization could make a significant difference if leaders could engage their highest level of thinking. His irreverence for the way things had been done in the past and his entrepreneurial zeal created the underlying principles of the Root Learning approach. The practices, experiments, and insights illustrated in this book stand on Randy's shoulders, and on his desire to integrate humanities with business disciplines. His goal was to tap the human spirit in order to achieve better results. Thank you, Randy.

The Art of Engagement has existed on the drawing board for more than 10 years. A team of people at Root Learning, guided by Christy Contardi Stone's outstanding leadership, has worked tirelessly to build outlines, develop proposals, write sample chapters, and edit and reedit drafts. The team has carried both the spirit and the content of the book from concept to completion. This truly talented and dedicated group represents nearly every team within Root, and includes Rich Berens, Lori Fournier, Brad Haudan, Veronica Hughes, David Kalman, Robin Wooddall Klein, Alison Lazenby, Heather Lee, Don MacLean, Gary Magenta, Emily Obereder, Karen Proffitt, Alma Reising, Tricia Richards, Erika Steiskal, and Victor Zhang.

Many friends and clients volunteered to read draft manuscripts, providing ideas, opinions, and recommendations to make sure we captured the energy and impact of Root Learning. To these special partners, a big thank you for generously sharing your real-world experiences. Your insights greatly improved the simplicity and practical application of how we communicated our ideas throughout the book. Thank you to Jim Anderson, Kirk Aubry, Lewis Campbell, Connie Colao, Tom Davin, Cyrus DeVere, Elaine Gregg, Hannah Kahn, Bob Lambert, Ken Matzick, Rich Meelia, Charlie Piscitello, Rob Savage, Jim Schleckser, Rich Teerlink, Sue Tsokris, James Webb, and Gina Valenti. I am especially grateful to Marcus Buckingham for his kind comments regarding *The Art of Engagement*.

Knox Huston of McGraw-Hill embodies everything anyone could ever want in an editor-coach. You encouraged us from the start to tell *our* story in *our* way. When we got off track, you helped us find our way back, and when we needed major rerouting, you made a memorable trip to Ohio to help us rediscover our confidence and simplify our story. Your depth of publishing knowledge, straightforward feedback, and warm, personable management style made writing the book a great experience.

Rich Berens's critical thinking and editorial insight appear throughout the book. Rich is one of the key architects of the Strategic Engagement Process, along with the thought partnership of Katie Outcalt. Rich is also the developer of the Strategic Engagement Index. As president of Root Learning, his contributions go beyond what is attributed in this book.

Victor Zhang, the lead illustrator, is a brilliantly talented artist who has perfected the skill of creating visual languages that inspire meaning. He is a master at telling complex stories through simple metaphors and images. He is equally gifted at applying both sides of his brain. Clients around the world have used the word "magical" to describe their experiences in working with Victor. All of the visuals in the book, including the book cover, were created by Victor and several members of his team, including Erika Steiskal, Michael Champion, Pat Cheal, and Ben Garrison. Lori Fournier provided significant graphic design leadership that is invaluable to telling the Root Learning story.

There would not be a book without the multi-talented Veronica Hughes. Veronica is an editor, poet, translator, motivator, and author. Somehow she scrubbed and polished my stream-of-consciousness ramblings into something that made sense. She tolerated five-minute breaks that turned into hour-long disappearances, and with her unique blend of urgency and patience, made sure that we never got too far behind. In the true spirit of the values of Root Learning, she was the servant-leader behind the scenes. She led by being of service and, in doing so, enabled the stories and concepts to be more succinct, more exciting, more connected, more inspirational, and more practical. Veronica, you are the "difference maker," a title that exceeds your role in bringing *The Art of Engagement* to life.

INTRODUCTION

L ike people, every company has a story—a journey that includes where it's been, where it is now, and where it wants to go. And like people, if the company is taking an *important* journey, it's helpful to have a map that charts the course to the desired destination. A company's strategy typically serves as this map. The strategy describes how the company plans to achieve its goals, to realize its dreams. That's why leaders of successful businesses spend a great deal of time making sure they create the perfect strategy. They do in-depth analyses, bring in consultants, book off-site meetings to escape daily demands, and work long hours on revisions until they feel it's *just right*.

Interestingly, when you talk to many of these leaders, they'll admit that developing the strategy is the easy part! They tell us that the challenging part, the place where they struggle the most, is in *executing* the strategy. Most of them are willing to show you their "strategy execution scars." They'll tell you about big meetings for communicating the strategy, PowerPoint presentations designed to rally the troops, measures of success for monitoring progress, and their high expectations for better business results. And when nothing changes, they're bewildered. They wonder, "Why aren't we better off than we were a year ago? Where did we go wrong? How can we get everyone on board? How do we get our people to think and act on our critical issues?"

Over the years, we've learned that *strategy execution* has the greatest impact on a company's success. Executives spend a wealth of time perfecting a strategy, but not nearly enough time planning its execution. As a result, they fail to achieve their goals and fail to make their organizational dreams come true.

This book is about what you can do to ensure that your strategies are executed . . . that you're able to translate aspirations into tangible results. It's about making all the hard work of strategy development pay off. *The Art of Engagement* shows how engaging your people in the execution of the strategy can catapult your business forward and create an energized workforce in the process.

So what exactly is it that prevents an organization from executing a strategy? We call it "the gap between people and possibilities." Truthfully, with most organizations, it's more of a canyon than a gap. In fact, *two* specific canyons tend to create the greatest challenges (the map below is shown in color at the center of the book).

The first canyon represents the gap that's created when a company tries to execute its strategy *despite* its people rather than *through* them. In an effort to drive ahead regardless of whether employees are on board, companies may attempt to execute their plans in a way that's not meaningful to their employees, as if they

Bridging disengagement and disconnection to reach the treasure.

haven't recognized that *human beings execute strategy*. The result? The "Disengagement Canyon," where we find large numbers of people who don't understand the strategy, aren't invested in bringing it to life, and certainly don't see the importance of their roles in executing it. Bridging this first canyon is done by connecting people to the strategy and making it theirs—though that doesn't necessarily connect them to each other.

The second canyon is formed by a company's failure to create a process that clearly outlines how the strategy will be executed and, most important, connects the people to each other in that execution. The "Disconnection Canyon" illustrates that, without a process, even people who understand and embrace a strategy can't achieve the intended results alone.

The good news is that bridges can be built over these canyons. We've been helping hundreds of companies (and millions of people) to do this for over 20 years, partnering with them to determine the best ways to engage their people with their strategy, and then to connect leaders, managers, and other individuals within the organization to each other so that their efforts form a framework that enables them to achieve their goals.

Through the words, pictures, and stories in this book, we'll share the art of connecting people to strategy—and to each other—to enable you to reach your destination.

Jim Haudan, CEO
Root Learning

What "Engagement" Really Means

1

What Do You Mean, You Want a Hot Dog?

I've been a lifelong fan of the Cleveland Indians baseball team. However, in the 1960s, '70s, '80s, and early '90s, the Indians' seasons were almost always over by Memorial Day. They were so bad so often that nobody objected when Hollywood made three baseball-spoof movies about the Indians—the *Major League* series. It just seemed natural to use the Indians as the poster children for inept performance. Unfortunately, my wife, Michelle, and my

"What do you mean, you want a hot dog?"

three children, Brad, Brooke, and Blake, adopted my loyalty to the Indians. Their experience of cheering for a winning team was limited, and their confidence in my ability to pick a winner was nonexistent.

Finally, in 1995, the Indians made it to the World Series for the first time in over 40 years. For the first World Series game in Cleveland that year, we were the absolute first people in the ballpark as they opened the gates. It was surreal! For all of us, there was a renewed sense of hope from being associated with a *winner*. The atmosphere was electric, and the game couldn't start soon enough. We felt as if we were personally related to the 42,000 fans who wore the same colors, cheered for the same players, and shared their predictions on the outcome of the game. We were high-fiving people we didn't know and even enjoyed the long lines for our pregame restroom visit. We were engaged. Captivated. We had something in common that brought us close together. We were all passionately rooting for the same thing—an Indians victory.

> **We were engaged. Captivated. We had something in common that brought us close together. We were all passionately rooting for the same thing—an Indians victory.**

As we passed through the crowd, we heard people from ages 8 to 80 talking about the "what-ifs." Row after row of Indian faithful were sharing opinions on the head-to-head starting pitchers and the next two or three pitching moves to make if something didn't go as planned. Who should be the first relief pitcher? Who should pinch-hit, and when? Which player should try to steal a base? The spirited conversation didn't just stick to Game 1—some fans were even looking at the key decisions of this game in light of the entire series, so we wouldn't lose sight of the big picture— winning the whole championship. Everyone was breathlessly awaiting the first World Series game in Cleveland in 40 years, and we were there in person!

We got to our seats just in time for the national anthem. I looked down our row and checked on the guests in our party—my family, a few neighbors, and two clients—young German executives from Mercedes-Benz. Moments later, the Indians took the field and set up in their defensive positions. Cleveland's pitcher completed his warm-up throws from the mound. We were ready for the first pitch! We weren't sitting on the edge of our seats—we were *standing* on them, screaming our lungs out for the Tribe.

At that exact moment, my guests from Germany asked if I would go to get them some hot dogs. I looked at them in utter disbelief. I couldn't believe what I said next. It went something like this:

"What do you *mean*, you want hot dogs? It's the first pitch of the World Series! I don't care how much money you spend with us—this is the first pitch of the *World Series*! Do you understand—the World Series! It doesn't get any bigger than this! My kids haven't had a chance to cheer for a winner ever, and tonight, for the first time in their baseball lives, they are on the side of a winner! With all due respect, just sit down and watch the ball game! How can you *possibly* think of food at a moment like this?"

My German guests sat down, a bit bewildered at my animated response. Then, sometime during the third inning, my neighbor tapped me on the shoulder and said, "I get it." I said, "You get what?"

"I get what you do for a living," he said. "I watched that conversation between you and your German clients. It all just came to life for me." I asked him to explain, and this is what he said.

"Right now there are about 42,000 people in the stands. I'd guess that 41,998 understand the game. They get the basic concept of the competition, they know about the skills that have been developed by both teams, and they are fully aware that the winner is the team that takes the best of seven games. These 41,998 people understand how the game is won. They know how to keep score and what is necessary to score. Even better, they realize what's needed to prevent the other team from scoring.

"Finally, they understand that the game strategy starts in the clubhouse before the game, when the manager fills out the lineup card. But all 41,998 people know that the lineup card is just the starting point—that after the first pitch, everything is in motion. And that drives a constant attempt to revise the strategy, switch players, develop and reexamine the plays that each team attempts to execute, and choose the next moves based on the changing momentum and events of the game.

"Oh, by the way, there are two guys here—at the first World Series game in Cleveland in 40 years—who don't have a clue. At the point of greatest excitement and drama, they are oblivious to what's going on, and they want to get hot dogs. Worse yet, they want *you* to get them hot dogs. There's a difference between just attending a game and being really involved in it. You're passionately engaged and want to participate in everything that's happening here. For them, it's just an interesting event that's festive, but pretty much meaningless. And that's why what happened gave me an insight about what you do to help organizations engage people in the game of their business."

As I thought about his comments, I realized that, in most organizations, we face just the opposite of what happened in the stands that day in Cleveland. We have 41,998 people who *don't* understand the game or how it's played. They don't understand the big picture of their business. They don't understand the competitive pressures created by the teams they play. They don't understand that the evolving customer expectations are swiftly changing what is valued or the critical balance between the short-term and longer-term issues that will determine whether they will be competing in the World Series or struggling to win more games than they lose.

Furthermore, they don't understand how we keep score, and they don't even know what the current score *is*. They have no idea where the money comes from or where it goes in their organization. They're not connected to the key levers that are used to execute financial performance.

The 41,998 people in most companies don't realize that the strategy isn't something that you place on home plate before the start of the game and then wait for things to play out. The strategy is in motion and must be adjusted continually to give us the best chance to win. All of the "what-ifs" must be constantly considered, and the essential struggles must be understood and taken on so everyone can continue to execute effectively.

> **The strategy is in motion and must be adjusted continually to give us the best chance to win.**

In business organizations every day, there are strategic struggles and captivating drama that would rival the juiciest soap operas, but people are tuned out. And just when many people can make one heck of a difference, at the moment when the things they do can really matter, at a time when the game is on the line . . . they go to get a hot dog. They miss being a part of something that has purpose and allows them to make a meaningful contribution to the execution of the company strategy.

If you don't think that people in most organizations are capable of getting into the strategic game of their business, consider this. All over the country, people are playing fantasy football, baseball, and basketball. They set up their teams and develop a strategy that they believe will be a winner. They buy and sell players, check their standings, evaluate the composition of their teams, and decide exactly when to play which players. They check the score and understand the metrics that point to a team weakness, and then make more moves to improve their chances of ultimate success. They are, without question, *in the game*.

The fundamental questions are these: If people of all ages and educational levels can get into the game of baseball to the extent that they can be "owners" and "managers" of fantasy teams and make decisions to determine their teams' destiny, why can't we get those 41,998 people in our businesses into the game?

Engagement means creating an energized "World Series" environment for our teams, so that people won't want to miss any part of the game—because the game is part of *them*. *The Art of Engagement* unlocks the lessons learned in more than 20 years of trial and error at engaging people in their companies' strategies. It shows exactly how to get people to forgo the hot dog and choose to get into the strategic games of their organizations so that they can be part of something bigger than themselves and will stand on their chairs screaming for their team to win!

There is a way to do this. It's called strategic engagement.

The Engaged Difference

Three bricklayers work side by side. Each one picks up a brick, spreads it with mortar, and sets it in place. A little boy asks them, "What are you doing?"

The first bricklayer says, "I'm putting one brick on top of another. Isn't that obvious?"

The second says, "I'm building a wall for the west side of a church."

The third says, "I'm creating a cathedral. It will stand for centuries and inspire people to do great deeds."

Laying a brick is a far cry from creating a cathedral.

This simple story has two key variables—the *approach* and the *outcome*. Consider these questions that deal with both approach and outcome:

Which bricklayer was just looking forward to quitting time?
Which one was focused only on his task or his part of the job?
Which bricklayer was truly engaged in what he was doing and understood the link between his work and the impact it would have on other people?

9

There is a wide variance between just laying a brick and building a cathedral. The approach and the results are dramatically different. This book explores that difference. It's about how to engage people to create better results.

"SEEING FORWARD"

Before we get into the "how-tos" (this *is* a how-to book), let me describe our journey at our company, Root Learning, and the mindset shift that landed us on the topic of engagement. We didn't start there, but it made such an impact that we've spent the last 20-plus years immersed in "the art of engagement."

> **There is a wide variance between just laying a brick and building a cathedral.**

In the early days, Root Learning was a publishing house. As part of our job, we spent massive amounts of time researching and writing about business trends. We'd often sit in a figurative hot-air balloon above an industry and analyze the societal, demographic, economic, organizational, and strategic trends that affected it. We had a knack for finding—and combining—obscure, emerging changes and confidently projecting these changes as "critical trends" to be reckoned with. We had a voracious appetite for spotting and understanding the major forces that were radically rearranging the business landscape. It was great fun to get paid to learn, and a real kick to be called futurists. We learned from Ted Levitt, former editor of the *Harvard Business Review*, that "the future belongs to people who see possibilities before they become obvious." A rallying cry began to emerge: If leaders and managers could "see what we see," they wouldn't be doing what they are doing! It was clearly all about what people could see, or in some cases, what they *couldn't* see.

An article in *Time* magazine that ran more than 20 years ago titled "Simply the Best" bolstered our convictions. It focused on two American athletes who were phenomenal performers, although they were both far from being the best athletes in their respective sports. The article explained how many other athletes possessed physical attributes and skills that were superior to those of these players, and yet these two—Larry Bird in basketball and Wayne Gretzky in hockey—were "simply the best." The general conclusion was that the two differentiating capabilities of these performers were exceptional anticipation and extraordinary peripheral vision. These insights convinced us even further that the road to superior performance had everything to do with how well a leader or manager at any level could "see forward." We were absolutely certain that if business executives could do this, they could lead their respective companies to the promised land. We began to put our convictions to the test.

At first, we consulted with business leaders on the creation of great strategies. Leaders of global companies brought us in to act as provocateurs at the front end of their planning process. Our charge was to help the senior team go on a "strategic road trip" that was focused on looking through the front windshield instead of in the rearview mirror. We usually convened our journey at some of the best resorts, golf courses, and wineries (our favorite). We started by challenging business leaders' thinking and examining how they viewed the future. Our mutual goal was to ride the winds of change rather than be blown away by them. We convinced ourselves that trends were the raw material for strategy, and that the best strategies—the strategies that would win—were the ones that would take advantage of those trends. Generally, after several days of intense work, we were aligned on the belief that we had nailed the most important issues for the company's future and that success was right around the corner. We concluded our sessions by toasting our collective brilliance in the cocktail lounge! Then, to be sure that our brilliance didn't sneak off in the weeks and months ahead, we dutifully captured our best thinking, our most important "from this to that" changes, and our vital next-step actions in several documents labeled "confidential." As a final touch, we packaged our documents in attractive binders with shiny gold corners.

However, time after time, our "see forward" strategic plans quickly lost their initial energy. We would return to see how the team's best ideas were being implemented and found them to be DOA—dead on arrival. This didn't happen just once or twice. It was commonplace. We soon came to realize that success did *not* actually depend on how masterfully a leader or manager could "see forward" or perceive the detailed nuances of a new strategy. It depended on successfully engaging the rest of the organization in understanding and acting on the conclusions that we had toasted—in simple terms, executing the strategy.

As a result of our new understanding, we developed an entirely new mind-set and a new principle: Success, competitiveness, and vitality were not determined by the laser-sharpness of the vision and strategy of the "brightest few" in a company, but by the learning, understanding, and execution speed of the "slowest many."

AN OUTSIDE-IN APPROACH TO LEARNING ABOUT ENGAGEMENT

Our passion changed from helping a few people to see the future to engaging the energy of an entire company. The new approach centered on democratizing strategic information and engaging people in the dramatic stories of the business. The real lever of success was not capturing the ideas of the leaders, but bringing these strategic ideas and issues to life in a language that made sense for *all* the employees of an organization.

So then, we faced a number of questions. How could we convince an entire organization to think and act differently? How could we encourage those discretionary efforts that are so critical to success? How could we get the full workforce to be engaged, thereby enabling a strategy to succeed? Our search began with trying to reach a deep understanding of the secrets of authentic and sustained engagement. We decided to start pursuing these questions, not in businesses, but in places where people were already engaged. Our goal was to then bring these discoveries back to the business environment.

The real lever of success was not capturing the ideas of the leaders, but bringing these strategic ideas and issues to life.

To answer our questions, we started with people—the true engines of business—because we were beginning to realize that engaging people was the key to strategy execution. Our goal was to find out what made aspects of individuals' lives so engaging and how we could apply this knowledge in a business environment. Here are some of the areas we explored (and continue to explore) for insights.

SPORTS FANATICS

What is it about sports that makes fans follow and truly care about their favorite teams? I've never seen a true fan of any sport checking a watch, falling asleep, counting the minutes until the game is over, or being bored out of his mind. (Compare this with any meeting you've recently attended.) Fans are acutely aware of what has transpired, keenly focused on what is currently going on, and contemplating what may happen next. The last thing they need to see are the words "Be Here Now" on the sign above the stands.

BEDTIME STORIES

What is it about a great bedtime story that engages the minds of our children? What is the secret that captivates and transports them to another place and time? What if we based our technique on "story time" to match today's business world? Try to put a child to bed by announcing that you're going to show her a PowerPoint deck! And if she displays any resistance at all, remind her that this is the *very latest* PowerPoint deck and that it has even more graphics and icons to help energize her imagination! Clearly, the outcome would not be pretty. What kids (and grown-ups) want is a character they can identify with and the ability to step into stories where a difficult journey brings them to gratifying success.

CONCERTS

What is it about rabid music fans that makes them do strange things in public just for the sake of sharing space with their favorite artists? Why do Parrotheads drive hundreds of miles dressed in Key West finery for the opportunity to live in Margaritaville for a few hours with Jimmy Buffett? What motivates otherwise sane people to stand and put their hands together to simulate "fins to the left, fins to the right" and sing "cheeseburger, cheeseburger" when, in fact, many of them avoid this food in normal life? There's something about being a real part of an event—if only for an evening.

DINNER WITH A FRIEND

What is it about having dinner with a close friend—where you start with "Good to see you!" and, before you know it, three or four hours have passed? Neither of you has any concept of time; you're completely immersed in thoughtful conversation. It's the kind of quality experience that makes you want more. Who cares whether the food was good? You didn't come for the food, but for the safety, excitement, and challenge of exploring personal issues with a close friend.

HARRY POTTER

What is it about the Harry Potter saga that inspires words like *pandemonium*, *obsession*, and *mania*? This "movement" broke every record for engagement. When Book 7 hit the streets in June 2007, it sold

8.3 million copies in 24 hours! This means 300,000 per hour, or more than 5,000 per minute—in the United States alone! What is it about this Harry guy, and what can we learn about engagement from his 10-year spell on the millions of people who could barely wait to read the next installment of his adventures? Imagine what would happen if business leaders could frame their company's journey as possessing the same adventure and intrigue as Harry Potter's. Could this offer that journey the same kind of magic?

So, magic spells aside, engagement comes down to tapping into the things that people really connect with, whether it's in sports, building cathedrals, speaking intimately with a friend, or Harry Potter. In the next chapter, we'll explore the four "roots of engagement" that move people from just showing up for a paycheck to truly participating in their company's strategy execution.

QUESTIONS FOR ACTION

1. *Consider the various aspects and facets of your life. What are the top activities in which you are engaged—activities during which time seems to fly by?*

2. *What is it that makes these activities so compelling that they capture your time, attention, and energy?*

3. *Can you use any of your insights about personal engagement to engage people in your organization?*

4. *What percentage of your people are putting one brick on top of another? What percentage are building a wall for a church? What percentage are creating a cathedral?*

3

The Roots of Engagement

Engagement is not one-dimensional. It's found in sports, friend-ship, and through all facets of life. It can be effortless, natural, and magnetic. Over the years, we've learned the characteristics of what really engages people in such a compelling, sustained way that they feel captivated, drawn in, and connected. We stumbled upon some of the "secrets to the sauce." We weren't present to interview those bricklayers who were building that cathedral. But

The roots of engagement.

People want to
...know that their contributions make a significant impact or difference.
...be a part of something big.
...feel a sense of belonging.
...go on a meaningful journey.

we have talked to some of the tens of millions of people we've helped to become more involved in the workings of their companies. We asked them what really engages them in their businesses—what's necessary for them to volunteer the contributions of their heads, hearts, and hands to their organizations.

There are four qualities that we keep hearing about that make engagement more natural. These qualities form the foundation or the roots of engaging people.

1. PEOPLE WANT TO BE A PART OF SOMETHING BIG. Who isn't interested in being a part of something that's bigger than themselves? It's evident in the way concertgoers act as one, connecting with hundreds of people they've never met in order to create a force far bigger than they could achieve by themselves. And by association, they feel like they're part of an effort, a piece of something more substantial and significant than they could ever be alone. When this happens, people get a feeling that *they are as big as the effort is.* This feeling affords a sense of substance, importance, pride, and direction.

You wouldn't think that country music legend Garth Brooks would feel the need to be part of something bigger than himself. (He's pretty big any way you look at it.) But in 2007, he was inspired by his wife, Trisha Yearwood, to join the fight against breast cancer. She took part in a 60-mile walk for the Susan G. Komen organization, the world's largest and most progressive grassroots network of cancer survivors and activists. Brooks said, "Of all the things my wife has done, I've never been more proud of her. So I started thinking, 'What can I do to be that cool?'"

Brooks produced a special "Pink Edition" of his *Ultimate Hits* album and donated $10 from the sale of each album to the fight against breast cancer, hoping to raise $10 million. When he released the album, he said, "This is the proudest day of my musical career."

The Komen organization's "main event," the Race for the Cure, has raised nearly $1 billion for breast cancer research in the past 25 years, and the color pink has become synonymous with breast cancer advocacy in everything from yogurt to jewelry. This group uses the power of more than 100,000 activists—including Garth Brooks—to bring about change at federal, state, and local levels.

What those people have accomplished is a result of "thinking big." It's impossible to get people in any organization to think big if they're constantly asked to "just do their job." They must understand the big-picture workings of the business and the overall purpose that it serves. Both of these contexts help people realize that what they can achieve with others is greater than what they could do by themselves.

> **It's impossible to get people in any organization to think big if they're constantly asked to "just do their job."**

In our experience, the universal joke is that leaders can just "mail in" the vision-mission-values statement, because every company needs to have one. And once it's created, organizations rarely do anything more about it. The beautifully printed document becomes tattered and torn, and eventually is posted on a wall next to the building evacuation plan. This important statement never achieves its greatest potential purpose—to connect people in organizations to something bigger than themselves. This isn't done by just writing a statement and then hanging it up or passing it out. The vision, mission, and values must be demonstrated by leaders and managers who bring them to life every day with the people they lead.

2. PEOPLE WANT TO FEEL A SENSE OF BELONGING. When people are truly engaged, they believe that they really belong. They have a sense of meaning or validation when they feel that they "fit," they're accepted, they're one of the group. It's a sense of affiliation and connection, and they can go forward together because they have something in common. On the other hand, a feeling of being on the outside, or not belonging, can disintegrate into something much worse than disengagement. Consider this story:

A little girl wants to play soccer. Her parents sign her up for a team and buy her the shin guards, shoes, and other equipment she needs to participate. They're excited about her upcoming practices and games. Through all the preseason practices, she enthusiastically does everything that the coach asks. She shows up for the first match, eager to get in the game, but the coach decides to keep her on the bench. Her parents feel bad for her, but assure her that if she tries harder, things will get better. They help her practice every night, working on foot skills and other soccer basics. At the next game, she's on the bench again. Although they're disappointed, the parents and little girl don't give up—instead, they set up a net in the backyard and practice even harder. Saturday comes again, and still she sits on the bench. The parents call the coach.

From enthusiastic to disillusioned to disengaged.

He suggests that she's not quite ready to play. At the next game, still no action. Then, the frustrated parents talk to others about the coach in terms that are less than polite. When other children play ahead of their daughter, they resent those children and their parents. They secretly hope that others may not show up for a future match—or that someone will twist an ankle so their little girl can play. Over the next few weeks, the parents and their daughter care less and less about how the team does. They are no longer connected to the team, the coach, or anyone associated with soccer. They are actively disengaged. This culminates midway through the season, when they actually cheer for their team to lose.

A feeling of being on the outside, or not belonging, can disintegrate into something much worse than disengagement.

I've told this story dozens of times to groups of leaders and managers, and then asked how many have experienced this kind of phenomenon. Every time, fully three-fourths of the audience say that they—or someone related to them—have gone through a situation where, slowly but surely, a well-intentioned parent and child have become disillusioned, then disengaged, and ultimately destructive to the team. Of course, this could happen with a theater group, a jazz ensemble, or a dance team—but the result is the same.

In an instant, the people in these audiences recalled how it felt to be disengaged or not belong. It's important to remember what it's like to start off being excited about a new job and a new role and, over time, become disillusioned because you don't feel that you can fully play.

In many companies, managers and frontline associates don't see where they belong in executing the strategy of the business. They may initially (and energetically) offer opinions and ideas; then, when their thoughts are ignored or disregarded, they slip into indifference. As in our soccer story, they start to distrust their leaders and become more aligned with those wearing the uniform of cynicism and apathy—the disengaged—than those who are actively working for the organization to win.

The people at Beaumont Hospitals in Michigan know the importance of feeling as if you belong. Not long ago, more than 13,000 employees met to share the organization's new vision. Ken Matzick, Beaumont's CEO, noticed that what happened that day went beyond communication of a unified message. The experience gave people a sense of belonging simply because they were asked to express their own ideas. "When leaders show respect by asking employees for their opinions," Matzick said, "people feel valued and connected, and see themselves belonging to the process of driving change."

3. PEOPLE WANT TO GO ON A MEANINGFUL JOURNEY. We all want to be on some kind of purposeful adventure that matters. As part of moving forward, there's a feeling of excitement, pioneering, discovery—and a sense of accomplishment that comes from achieving something that matters. It's more than attractive; it's downright heady. It's the part of the human spirit that suggests we can be more, that we are more. Robert Redford was once asked why he continued to support the Sundance Institute for fledgling filmmakers. He said, "I've always operated from a belief that if we could do more, we should." We all want to create something that doesn't exist right now. Nobody wants to sum up a lifetime by saying, "I did one hell of a job maintaining what was already there." What's important is, "Here's what it was like when I arrived, and here's how I made it better!" Our journey is both a challenge and an opportunity that compels us to take risks and makes overcoming the barriers worth the effort.

Some journeys are more public than others. In the mid-1980s, Chrysler, a longtime mainstay of the American auto market, was flirting with insolvency. After a long struggle, the U.S. government stepped in to provide financial backing. Chrysler was given a federal guaranteed loan that the company was to pay back when the storm was over. I spent a day with a senior engineer at Chrysler a few years later, and he gave me the inside story. Here's what he told me:

"When Chrysler got those loan guarantees, this was an amazing place to work. Everybody on the outside thought we were on life support, but nothing could have been further from the truth! All of us who worked here shared a spirit of commitment—there was no way we'd let down our country or our company. We were absolutely certain about this. It was like an adventure, like a pledge we were going to fulfill. You could come in here at any time of the day or night and find lights on in the offices. If anyone asked for help, anywhere, they got it instantly. All our bureaucracies melted. It didn't matter what department you worked in, somebody was always ready to pitch in and do whatever it took to get the job done. It was a real journey of pride to pay back the government that had shown such faith in us. We had a shared direction and we were all totally involved in it."

Then he said something surprising. "I can tell you the month, the week, the day, heck, the minute that we paid back the last dollar we owed to the government," he said. "It was like somebody had taken a hammer and smashed this place. The adventure was over, and there wasn't a new one to take its place in the hearts of the people here at Chrysler. This was the sad beginning of a significant decline in the performance of our business. In my mind, that absence of a compelling adventure was what kept people from creating a better company that could sustain itself over time. It was all about a purpose, a challenge to prove that we were worthy, that the trust extended to us was well placed."

As we know, Chrysler went through several years of trying to regain its reputation for excellence, and then was sold and resold.

Nothing to date has reclaimed that sense of adventure that propelled it during those tough years.

In simple terms, a strategy is an adventure. And a meaningful strategy captures a sense of purpose, of doing something together that is worth the effort. It creates incredible energy and a formidable challenge, and it unites people in the pursuit of outstanding achievement. This sense of adventure with purpose is a far cry from the jargonized rhetoric frequently heard in the strategy presentations that have become a mainstay in many organizations. Time after time, people we've worked with don't know the score of the game or the status of the adventure. They really don't realize what they're up against, where they stand, and what they're trying to accomplish as a business. When they understand the real challenges they face in the quest, they don't have to be coerced to be engaged. The presence of "good and evil" in the story motivates them to try to win.

4. PEOPLE WANT TO KNOW THAT THEIR CONTRIBUTIONS MAKE A SIGNIFICANT IMPACT OR DIFFERENCE. People want to be written into the story, to know that what they do really makes a difference, especially in the lives of other people. This applies to all other areas of life as well as to business. If I'm there, I'm part of the story. It's different because of me. In Chapter 2, we noted that when people dress up in tropical clothes and sing "Margaritaville," they feel that they're making the concert a greater experience for everyone, that what they're doing is connected to the outcome of the event. And in the same way, that little old lady watching a game on TV with her baseball cap on backwards really believes she's helping a rookie hit a home run.

If you've ever seen the midday parade down Main Street at Disney's Magic Kingdom, you may have witnessed some of Disney's senior leadership disguised as Donald Duck or Captain Hook. Whenever new executives join the staff at the Magic

Kingdom, they're required to participate in the parade. The reason: to see firsthand how what they do is reflected in the eyes of children. At a recent meeting, a senior leader at Disney told me that the organization wants to impress upon new executives that there is a direct connection between their daily work and the magic they create for people. He said, "You can't take off that costume without feeling awe, wonder, amazement, and knowing that you made a difference in the lives of others."

> **Engaged people feel that whatever they're doing is unquestionably connected to making a difference in the lives of other people.**

Engaged people feel that whatever they're doing is unquestionably connected to making a difference in the lives of other people. If he's engaged, the librarian who repairs books believes that he's saving history for future generations. The hotel employee who sets up the breakfast bar believes that she's helping the businessperson prepare for a successful day.

Whether in our conversations with employees around the world or our observations of daily life where people are truly engaged, we found that engagement involves these four characteristics. When people believe they are part of something big, feel like they belong, feel they are on a meaningful journey, and can see how they are helping to make a difference, engagement occurs naturally—even in business.

QUESTIONS FOR ACTION

1. *Consider your most important strategic initiatives. As you engage people to execute these initiatives, do you think they know:*
   - *That they are part of something bigger than themselves?*
   - *That they truly belong?*

- *That they're on a meaningful adventure?*

- *And that their contributions make a significant difference?*

2. *The bricklayer who built the cathedral in the previous chapter knew that he was part of something bigger than himself. How could you help people see the bigger picture of what they do?*

3. *How many people in your organization are silently cheering for you to lose? If the slippery slope of disengagement starts in the alienation between the player and coach, what can you do to let people know that they belong even if they're not ready to take the field?*

4. *If you were to transform your strategy and performance targets into an adventure tale, what is the victory (other than financial) that you would win?*

5. *How can you give your employees an experience equal to marching down Main Street as a Disney character so they can see the wonder in the eyes of the people who benefit from their contributions?*

The
Disengagement Canyon:
Voices from the
Trenches

*I*n Part 1, we explored the meaning of true engagement, and it seems pretty straightforward. People work because they have to. That's why they call it "work." But people engage only when they want to. And the core of unlocking that desire is recognizing the role that leaders, managers, and organizations play in artfully tapping into the discretionary efforts of human beings. People spend more than 40 percent of their waking hours every week going through the motions in the organizations that cut their paychecks. The opportunity is to convert these motions into the emotions that people feel when they have a chance to be a part of something bigger than themselves, when they know that they really belong in their organization, when they are immersed in a meaningful adventure, and when they know that their contributions make a significant difference.

But making this happen in the workplace is not so straightforward. The "canyon" is the reality of business today. In Part 2, we'll talk about the reasons why people are disengaged. Together, these reasons form the Disengagement Canyon.

The next six chapters are titled as "voices from the trenches," presenting the issues that people have told us are preventing them from truly engaging and committing to their organizations.

4

I Can't Be Engaged
If I'm Overwhelmed

When we think of "not being overwhelmed," the word *simple* comes to mind. But simple is not easy. Mark Twain once said, "I'd have written a shorter letter if I'd had more time," and many others have expressed the same sentiment. A course in effective letter writing might help us all simplify the complex strategies we create. Employees are the recipients of many strategic "letters"—in the form of edicts, memos, and other dictates—that often rain down on them without rhyme or reason. When leaders tell employees that *everything* is important, nothing sticks or really matters. But while simplicity is not easy, it's essential to engagement.

Let's look at an example. A restaurant manager at Taco Bell once created a collage from several months' worth of company directives—standards, new slogans, promotions, and performance updates. When the manager showed the collage to his leaders, it made a huge impression! It took the Taco Bell leaders just a glance to see that communication had become overwhelming and that it was impossible to make sense of this barrage of orders. Unfortunately, in most instances, the norm is to just add one more paper to the pile. What results is complexity, confusion, and conflict, which in turn cause most people to spend the majority of the day figuring out how to survive instead of how to meaningfully contribute.

REACTING PREVENTS ENGAGEMENT

Near the end of his life, management guru Peter Drucker responded to a question that went something like this: "What one thing would you ask a leader or manager to determine how effective he or she was?" Drucker's answer was brief and to the point. He said, "I would ask them what they've stopped doing in the last two months." Drucker was referring to the expansion of many business priorities, to a point that the pure volume of commands

> **M**ost people spend the majority of the day figuring out how to survive instead of how to meaningfully contribute.

was making employees feel overwhelmed. In a recent conversation I had, this theme resurfaced. An executive asked me, "How do we take away the previous 20 years of strategic directives to add the new?" I had never considered before that *stop* could be a much more important word than *start*.

But to the manager who made the collage, that's the problem! Leaders don't stop. Leaders don't remove. Leaders just add to the things they expect to be done, and then are surprised that people feel hopeless and disengaged. It's just not possible to feel engaged when people at all levels of the company are in a constant state of "whack-a-mole." We knock one thing down and another pops up.

Take a look at the whack-a-mole sketch on the next page. While whack-a-mole can be an exciting challenge to a child, it creates utter frustration for adults trying to manage a business in the same fashion. Individuals are left to be completely reactive, and they feel as if they've lost control. Employees are at the mercy of the next issue, or "mole," that pops into view. In business, moles represent a mixture of new strategies or priorities and old initiatives. It's the combination of these that creates the sense of being overwhelmed. The frustration is that we keep adding and never take anything away. Something has to give.

This is the exact sentiment that was described several years ago at Taco Bell—and this was a widespread problem. Rob Savage, Taco Bell's COO, explained that general managers are the chief links between the company leaders and the team members in the individual restaurants. General managers didn't have the ability to engage people in the business of their restaurants because they were spending too much time reacting to the latest corporate directives. "You can't execute new strategy if you don't remove some of the past," Savage said. "If your answer to 'What have you stopped doing?' is 'Nothing,' then it's impossible to be meaningfully engaged. What is interesting is that the *stop* activities must be just as deliberate and intense as the *start* actions. This is a whole new way of thinking for us."

As a result of this, Savage led a process to create one simple operating system that required the leaders across all functions in the business to be much more proactive in prioritizing, integrating, and simplifying the requests of managers in the organization.

How can company leaders ask general managers to focus more effort on building revenue and developing people if they aren't willing to allow managers to back off on some of the past priorities that no longer matter? When companies stop any processes, actions, or behaviors, they inevitably provide their employees with greater clarity and simplicity of purpose. Not only do they help their people connect the dots again, but the people have *fewer dots to connect*.

"I can't carry one more strategy!"

When we've helped Fortune 500 companies to clarify and simplify their strategies so that employees could understand where the company was headed, we've discovered that the remnants of old strategies are fundamentally barring companies from successfully launching new initiatives. These old strategies are the equivalent of "organizational cholesterol," which, if left alone, creates a blockage that makes any kind of strenuous new activity impossible. When people aren't free to hunt down and eliminate actions or activities that are duplicated,

> **When companies stop any actions, they inevitably provide their employees with greater clarity and simplicity of purpose.**

redundant, no longer add value, or are getting in the way of doing the job effectively, there's never any relief! Without leadership's permission to remove the burdens, the whack-a-mole way of life continues, and more and more moles keep popping up.

DESIGNED BY EXPERTS, INTENDED FOR NOVICES

In addition to having too much to do, people are often overwhelmed because strategy communication is rarely designed with the user in mind. Donald Norman's *The Design of Everyday Things* examines the concept of simple design in our daily lives. As a cognitive scientist, Norman studied the hidden frustrations resulting from problems that occur with seemingly simple objects. In his book, he chronicles the hardships he suffered in wrestling with difficult doors, perplexing light switches, baffling shower controls, plastic bags that can be opened only with your teeth, and car radios with innumerable buttons that all look the same and that can't be operated while you are actually driving your car. This frustration sparked his interest in human error.

After the 1979 disaster at Three Mile Island, the worst nuclear accident in U.S. history, Norman was among a group of scientists asked to investigate why the control room operators had made such terrible mistakes before and during the crisis. To his surprise, the findings didn't place the blame with the operators, but with the *design of the control room*. Similarly, when company strategies fail, the fault does not usually lie with the disengaged managers and individuals charged with implementing the strategy, but with leaders' design for engaging these people in the critical imperatives of the organization's future.

To be clear and understandable, a strategy needs to be simple. But most strategies we create are *not* simple, because the creators (the strategy makers) have forgotten what it's like not to know. When it comes to engaging others, it's very difficult for leaders not to be influenced by their own knowledge. Even worse, they can tell stories about a journey that only they experienced and assume it's just as enticing for others. It's like watching a slide show of a friend's vacation. If your friend shows you pictures of every meal and museum, it's painful. Similarly, the sentiment of the leaders is often, "We get it, so everybody else should too!" What leaders forget is how long it took them to get it, and why it's necessary to go back to square one in making it simple for others. This isn't about dumbing down the strategy, but about making it sophisticated, elegant, and brilliantly simple so less experienced people can instantly grasp its meaning.

Business leaders are not alone in forgetting that they need to meet people where they are rather than where leaders would like them to be. Manufacturers of DVD players, digital cameras, and electronic appliances have cornered the market on creating products that confuse even the most savvy consumers. The user struggles to work with a dizzying array of features that mystify and confuse when they'd have no problems with a straightforward display of basic and intuitive buttons and dials.

So, the point of this chapter is to show the need for leaders to eliminate the feeling that there's too much to do and it's too confusing that usually result from leaders not actively seeking out and discontinuing old ways of doing business. No one can be meaningfully engaged if they're constantly whacking a herd of moles.

QUESTIONS FOR ACTION

1. *What have you, your organization, or your team stopped doing in the last two months to create capacity so your employees can focus on new strategies, actions, and behaviors?*

2. *What would your whack-a-mole sketch look like? (For a blank sketch to start with, go to www.rootsofengagement.com.) What are all the initiatives or requests that you could label to personalize the sketch? Which of these are really remnants of past strategies that get in the way?*

3. *Are you designing your strategic communications for the "engineers" or the "users"? Businesses test new products and services with focus groups. What could you do to test the design of your strategic communications to be sure they make sense to the users?*

4. *How overwhelmed do you think your people are? How much is this feeling affecting their level of engagement? What could you do to better integrate, simplify, or clarify?*

5

I Can't Be Engaged
If I Don't Get It

In classic strategy-speak, an executive once said, "These tests were conducted over a six-month period using a double-blind format of eight overlapping demographic groups. Every region of the country was sampled, and the focus testing of our toys showed a solid base in the 9-to-11-year-old bracket with a possible carryover into the 12-year-olds. When you consider that Nobots and Transformers pull over 37 percent market share, and that we're targeting the same area, I think that we should see one-quarter of that, and that is one-fifth of the total revenue from all of last year. Any questions?"

Relevance can reawaken a childlike sense of discovery.

If you've seen the movie *Big*, you may remember this scene, and what happens next. "I don't get it," says Josh Baskin, played by Tom Hanks. Josh is an 8-year-old boy in the body of a man, but since he's a little kid at heart, he's far more relevant to the toy market than a grown-up. Josh took the leaders of the toy company on an interesting cultural journey of rediscovering what was relevant to its customers. In one memorable scene, Josh danced with the CEO on a giant electronic piano, playing "Chopsticks" and "Heart and Soul." With the inspired mind of a child in a toy factory, Josh became the company's wunderkind. His wide-eyed honesty and relevance were exactly the push the company needed.

> **If businesses can't be relevant in the eyes of the people who work for them, there's no way that they can "get it."**

There are two lessons to be learned from this scene. First, when businesses' products or services regain relevance in the eyes of their customers, they can be tremendously successful. Second, if businesses can't be relevant in the eyes of the people who work for them, there's no way that they can "get it."

WHO BRINGS THE RELEVANCE?

Relevance is at the heart of engagement; it's the sweet spot that makes the difference in helping people feel as if they belong. Consider a profession where relevance causes a person to instantly succeed or fail—stand-up comedy. When an audience believes that a comedian and his material are relevant to them, they're immediately engaged. They laugh, they're animated, and their energy engulfs the room. Compare this with the unlucky guy who bombs, gets heckled, and is booed off the stage. What he's doing and saying is just not funny because he establishes no association with the audience. They simply don't get it.

So whose responsibility is it to bring relevance to the engagement of others? In a former career as an educator, I once spoke with a veteran teacher about her curriculum. "How do you decide what to teach?" I asked.

She replied, "Well, I teach what they tell me to teach."

"No, really," I continued. "How do you decide what to teach?"

"There are state standards, district standards, the grade level— all these things tell me what I have to teach," she said.

I still wasn't satisfied. I asked again and again until I got what I felt was an honest answer. She said, "I teach what I like."

My follow-up questions were, "So what if what you like isn't what your students like? If we all teach what we like, whose role is it to bring the relevance of learning to the students?"

The teacher was unfazed by my sense that it was *her* role to uncover relevance rather than to expect the students to bring it. In the same way, the role of a leader is to focus on what is meaningful to the employee.

So I decided to put the teacher's comments and my beliefs to the test. The next day, I was driving my son Blake, then in the fifth grade, to basketball practice. "What did you learn in school today?" I asked.

"Nothing," he replied. "We just did busy work."

"What do you mean?" I asked.

"Well, the teacher didn't know what to do with us, so he showed us a movie," he said. "It kept us busy, but we didn't learn anything."

My theory about whose role it was to uncover relevance came to mind. "Blake," I said, "what are you curious about?"

He thought a moment and then said, "How does Caller ID know who's calling?"

I said, "I don't know. I'll get back to you on that. What else are you curious about?"

"Well, where does the color come from in clear bubble bath?"

Again I said, "I don't know. I'll get back to you on that one too. What else are you curious about?"

As interesting as his first two questions were, the third one blew me away. My fifth-grader said, "Well, Dad, as you go higher, there's less oxygen, right?"

"Yes," I said.

"And when you make a fire," he said, "you need oxygen for the fire to burn."

I had no idea where he was going, but I nodded in agreement.

"So," he asked, "if the sun is so high and there's no oxygen up there, how come it burns so brightly?"

As I pondered this question, I couldn't imagine a more engaging and enticing way to design a curriculum for any age than by starting with *what students are curious about*.

> **When leaders don't uncover what people are curious about in their work, a huge opportunity to help them get it is lost.**

What does all this have to do with business? We need to ask people what they're curious about, and what they want to know. When this has actually happened, we've heard some of the most profound questions that business leaders could hope for. When leaders can capture people's imagination, curiosity, and questions, they engage employees in an entirely new, exciting way. However, when leaders don't uncover and really understand what people are curious about in their work, a huge opportunity to help them get it is lost.

TWO WELL-KNOWN MASTERS OF RELEVANCE

Randy Root, my former partner, often spoke about two leaders who built businesses around relevance—Albert Kanter and Walt Disney. They used different techniques to unlock great content and make it accessible and understandable for large numbers of people.

From 1941 to 1971, *Classics Illustrated* (which most people know by its original name, *Classic Comics*) introduced baby boomers, soldiers, and kids of all ages to the stories of the world's greatest authors. Albert Kanter, the originator of the series, had a simple dream—to make these treasures available to the masses. He adapted and illustrated them, and then published them in comic book form, a medium that was already commonplace. By the mid-1950s, he had released over 100 titles in more than 20 languages, including Homer's *Odyssey*, Shakespeare's *Hamlet*, and biographies of Abraham Lincoln and Davy Crockett. The essence of his success was that the *Classics Illustrated* adaptors and illustrators retold timeless and exciting stories. The "translation" was an art in itself. All of us who loved these little gems had much the same experience: we could lose ourselves in tales told in a way that we could understand, no matter how complicated the plot or how many characters there were.

Let's look at another example. Just under 80 years ago, nobody had ever heard of Walt Disney, but since 1928, his work has been part of global culture. Like Kanter, Disney "translated" great stories—fairy tales—that were, at the time, somewhat obscure. He liberated the stories by adding motion and animation that brought them to life. In making the characters move, talk, and sing, he added a whole new element to the lives of generations of children and parents everywhere. The Disney magic continues, and for good reason—we can understand and connect with the stories. In drawing characters and animating them, he "drew in" people of all ages from all around the world. Both Kanter and Disney were masters of relevance because they translated the material for their audiences.

PEOPLE WON'T "GET IT" IF LEADERS DON'T ACT AS TRANSLATORS

Just like the teacher who teaches students "what she likes," leaders fall into the same trap of irrelevance when they communicate what makes sense only to them. Rather than creating a strategy that is so elegantly simple that everyone can understand and execute it, most leaders write strategy in a language that only a few can speak. They invent terms like "burning platform," "strategic plank," or "vital focus area." In many ways, leaders are writing the code for a special language that everyone else struggles to understand.

As a result, the leader's role as translator ends only when people truly get it. The role of translator is probably one of the least understood by leaders and managers. Indeed, in our years of working with hundreds of companies, the two most frequently spoken lines we've heard throughout an organization are "I don't understand what I should do differently" and "I don't know what I need to do to contribute." In terms of engagement, a leader has failed to translate the strategy into the appropriate future actions.

The essential task of a leader as translator is to literally and figuratively draw out and illustrate for employees all of the drama of the business. This includes the current business environment, the specifics of the marketplace, its customers, its competition, and its main strategies. Then, it becomes an exciting story that can be as clear and engaging as a volume of *Classics Illustrated*.

In addition, leaders need to constantly bring motion to the illustrations they create. The idea is to enable people to see cause and effect—how the strategy works, where it's going, the key links, and what's needed to make all the pieces work together. Adding movement shows that the strategy is not static, that it moves with the changes in the business and the needs of the customers.

QUESTIONS FOR ACTION

1. *How effectively are you using relevance when you try to engage your people? (In other words, if you were a comedian, would they laugh, or would you bomb?)*

2. *If Josh (Tom Hanks) were sitting in your strategy room, would he "get it"? What could you do to ensure that your strategic "pablum" is fit for employee consumption?*

3. When did you last ask your people what they're most curious about in your business? What do you think your people are curious about? How could you find out?

4. What are you curious about in your business, and how are you pursuing that curiosity?

5. In a Classics Illustrated- or Disney-like manner, how could you translate the exciting stories of your business?

chapter

6

I Can't Be Engaged
If I'm Scared

You may have heard of Abraham Maslow's hierarchy of needs. It's a model that the psychologist created in the 1940s that helps explain what motivates human beings. At the base are the indispensable *physical* needs: oxygen, food, and water. Ranking just above these is the most basic *psychological* need: the need to feel safe.

When we don't feel safe, fear drives our actions and interactions. Fear causes us to not be ourselves as individuals. In organizations, fear holds us back from performing at the level we're capable of. When we're afraid, we're guarded, cautious, and restrained, and we do everything we can to regain a feeling of security.

THE FREEDOM OF FEELING SAFE

The fear of not being liked or not being accepted influences many of us. It starts at a young age in the form of peer pressure.

When I was a high school administrator, I noted the excitement and energy of the freshmen every fall. So many had aspirations to play varsity sports, to star in the play, or to be elected to student council. They couldn't wait to contribute their talents. By midyear, some had reached their goals, but many had not. Some of the kids who fell short of their goals ended up in the detention hall as their frustration led to acting out. As their hopes to fit in dimmed, they moved from occasional detention hall visitor to standing member. Some progressed down the path to probation, absolutely-the-last-chance probation, and finally to expulsion. Fear of "never making the cut" kicked in and the students felt that they weren't talented enough to be a real part of the school. When this happened, they "signed up" for the easiest group to join—those who were against everything. This was a sad process to watch.

As a result, we started an intramural program with no tryouts or elections required. The activities included an overnight canoe trip. One year, one of the "problem kids" decided to go. On the ride to the canoe livery, he acted his part, being obstinate and mouthy. When we arrived, he continued to be disruptive.

By some strange twist of fate, he was assigned to my canoe. This is where fear-based peer pressure and the power of feeling safe converged. As we launched our canoe, he continued to show plenty of bad attitude. But then, we rounded a bend in the river and were suddenly alone. Within seconds, this high school tough guy transformed into a curious child, enchanted by the natural wonders he saw. He was no longer afraid of what others thought of him. He was fascinated as he watched trout jumping in the river and deer wandering near the shoreline. He began to ask questions—and the questions kept coming. This happy kid full of wonder was a stark contrast to the juvenile-delinquent-in-training who had boarded the canoe back at the launch. That student who behaved in the way he thought his peers expected—like a troublemaker—became who he really was when fear fell away.

So what does a 15-year-old who was cut from the basketball team, who became a detention hall resident, and then came alive as an enthusiastic naturalist on a canoe ride have to do with business? Everything.

Driven by peer pressure, adolescents frequently give up who they really are because of the fear of not fitting in and not belonging. In the same way, organizations can create a sense of "fear pressure" that has the same outcome—people avoid being who they genuinely are because they fear they won't be approved of or valued or that they'll do something wrong. Each situation is dangerous because the true talents and abilities of people are suppressed, resulting in disengagement, lack of execution, and failure to live up to their potential.

At the high school, we created an opportunity for kids to interact in an environment where they could be themselves. In organizations, leaders need to create environments where people can act authentically without fear of rejection or judgment. In doing so, an individual's talents and abilities will be allowed to flourish.

WHAT ARE PEOPLE SCARED OF?

When we ask people what they are afraid of at work, here's what they tell us:

- We're afraid that our contributions aren't really valued.
- We're afraid that our personal beliefs don't align with those of the company.
- We're afraid that we won't be able to adapt to changes in the way we work.
- We're afraid that we won't have a safe place to practice new skills.
- We don't feel that it's safe to fail and learn from failures.
- We don't feel that it's safe to say what we really think.
- We don't think it's safe to suggest better ways of doing things.
- We don't know how to disagree and not become branded "a problem."

With frameworks of rules, policies, and requirements, organizations create environments where people perceive that they must behave, think, and believe in a certain way. They fear that if they don't, they won't fit in, and there will be negative repercussions.

THE SAFE TIME OF THE WEEK

There are places where people *do* feel safe, where they simply do their best and let it stand for what it is rather than worry about how it will be perceived by others. This happens on weekends. Consider this: if each person's work is a series of self-portraits, most of the best pictures are painted on weekends and evenings after work.

In my experience, people *want* to go to work feeling as if they are making a difference. Yet, survival is often the primary objective. Shifting external forces, complexity, specialization, outsourcing, and segmentation in the workplace continue to intensify the fear of not being adequate or valuable enough for the future.

Employees are drowning in their own protective actions while starving for the safety that they find in the evenings and on week-

Putting on "work armor" for the day ahead.

ends when they know that they contribute to something mean-ingful (families or personal lives), when they have a sense of being needed (volunteer organizations), and when they know that their decisions impact their outcomes (fantasy football teams).

In these safe situations, fear doesn't cause them to act out in defiance, hold anything back, abandon their true beliefs, or go after any of their goals halfheartedly.

MAKING IT SAFE TO DISCUSS THE HARD ISSUES

In practicing the art of engagement, leaders have to recognize that what they're ultimately trying to do is engage *human beings*. But until people truly feel safe, leaders can't expect them to engage and perform at a higher level. Once leaders acknowledge that most organizations create rules that prevent people from being their true selves, they must break down the barriers and make it safe for employees to discuss the hard issues.

Creating a safe way to share ideas was a recent challenge for major retailer PETCO. Once at the top of the lucrative pet industry, PETCO had lost its position due to intense, diverse competition. Its leadership initiated a companywide transforma-tion in an effort to regain the top spot. To help in this transfor-mation, they decided to inform employees about the changing marketplace and the plan to retake the lead. The goal was to make it safe to talk about PETCO's current failing position and then to liberate the talent in the organization to act in a much more fearless way.

Charlie Piscitello, PETCO's senior vice president of human resources, said, "We had stopped listening to people in the field. As a result, they'd stopped telling us what they really thought."

The transformation process began with addressing this reality. PETCO brought many of its people together in small groups and endorsed a candid discussion about industry trends and PETCO's plan of action. The results were gratifying. "It was a great start," said Piscitello. "The process of encouraging people to say what they really think gave our people hope when they had despair. Our employees came out of the sessions knowing the company's plan, realizing that the company was trying hard to do the right thing, understanding how much they mattered, and seeing how they could influence the outcome. They went from despair to hope, and hope to belief. Now they can use that belief to act."

Piscitello asked his people for reactions to this new approach. A typical response was, "Normally, I'm fearful that if I don't give the right answer, I'll be ostracized or I'll feel stupid. Here, I didn't have the right answer, but I wasn't worried about speaking up because I felt like we were searching together."

Through all this, we learned that people won't explore or take risks unless they feel safe. When people aren't encouraged to search together, fear grows and the chances of finding solutions to an organizational problem shrink.

FORMALITY REINFORCES FEAR

Management expert Larry Bossidy tells us that "realism is at the heart of execution." He also says that to be real, you have to be candid, and that formality decreases candor.

Many of the formal aspects of our workplaces are reflections of the rules and procedures that define the culture of the business. In some companies, only certain employees are considered valuable. If the title on your business card doesn't place you at a certain level, you aren't invited into the strategy conversations. It's about the ability to play a part, not the ability to think. This forced formality perpetuates fear, uncertainty, and self-doubt.

In my first professional job, I worked in a school office with many seasoned veterans. One of my boss's first directions was, "Whatever you do, don't tell anybody that you're 21 and your bachelor's degree is in recreation." I grew a mustache simply because I was afraid that my colleagues would perceive me as inexperienced. I believed I needed to play the role and look the part.

Strangely enough, some 30 years later, after working with dozens of senior teams at Global 500 companies, I've found that most of those organizations are "growing mustaches" for their own reasons. The mustaches come in the form of stilted conversations, boring and lifeless business reviews, never-go-off-the-agenda meetings, and avoiding the elephant-in-the-room issues—all of which build an environment of anxiety.

Left to their own devices, people tend to succumb to peer pressure rather than *peer dialogue*. They may become unwilling to say things that might be wrong or to be vulnerable in front of each other. Without a level of informality in the workplace, fear and caution take over and cause people to fall short of what they're capable of achieving.

> **W**ithout a level of informality in the workplace, fear and caution take over and cause people to fall short of what they're capable of achieving.

Leaders need to remember that *human beings* work for them, and human beings need to feel safe. When employees don't feel safe, all of our actions and behaviors are concentrated on finding a safe place. Unfortunately, most organizations seem to be very good at building and sustaining fear pressure. So how can anyone be surprised that disengagement is such a common outcome?

QUESTIONS FOR ACTION

1. *How safe do your people feel about saying in public what they really believe?*

2. *How would you assess the gap between the engagement and creativity of your people on weekends versus during the week?*

3. *Are your people afraid of not being adequate or valuable for the future? How strong is that fear?*

4. *Is most of the energy of your people vested in protective actions and "growing mustaches" or in taking the risks necessary to elevate performance?*

5. *How well are you doing at giving permission to not be afraid and creating an informal environment?*

I Can't Be Engaged If
I Don't See the Big Picture

A CEO once asked a frontline associate her opinion of the organization. "The leaders are all messed up. I don't trust them," the associate said.

"Why?" the leader asked. "What do you see?"

She replied, "Well, I used to see complete incompetence. We got all this flavor-of-the-month stuff. We figured that the leaders

Without a picture, it's hard to fit the pieces together.

were trying to please each other or someone other than us—the people who do the work! We just assumed that leaders couldn't agree on what came next."

She continued, "Now, I see that the leaders don't do this on purpose. They're just not very good at helping us understand things. They use terms that we don't know, like CRM, TQM, ERP, supply chain, lean, and Kaizen. They assume that we know where and how these connect. It's as if they have a thousand-piece jigsaw puzzle, and they keep sending us all these pieces one at a time! And the pieces don't seem to belong together. One piece says 'Innovate,' and another says 'Cut costs.' One says 'Go slow' and another says 'Go fast.' One piece says 'Delight customers' and another says 'Reduce inventory.' Not a week goes by when we don't get a couple of more pieces, often the opposite of the previous month's bunch, with jagged edges that look impossible to fit together. After months of laying out all these pieces on our worktable, the only thing we can conclude is that they didn't all come from the same puzzle box.

"Why can't the leaders just send the box top across the table so we can see how all the pieces fit together? Is it really that hard to understand? I wonder how long the leaders would keep trying to assemble a puzzle if they had hundreds of little pieces and no clue about how they fit together or a picture of what they were building! They'd give up, and that's what most of the people in my department end up doing. Instead of trying to connect the pieces and figure out how to make sense of it all, we just stop and wait to be told what to do next. The feeling around here is that we can't make sense of the whole thing if we only see the pieces. Why don't the leaders just give us the cover of the puzzle box for our business?"

The puzzle story illustrates the challenge that many businesses face in getting people to see the picture from the biggest view possible. In simple terms, the "big picture" is the entire perspective of the business and all its issues, taking everything into account and seeing how it all connects. No credible company wants a sign over their front door that says, "We think *little* here." Yet that's exactly what happens, in three important ways.

1. THE IMPACT OF NOT THINKING BIG AT A SYSTEMS LEVEL

A company needs to help people think about its systems. A system is basically a group of steps or related elements that, when organized, makes up a complex whole. It's a map that tells us where we are and how to get where we want to go.

Let's consider an easy model—the U.S. highway system and its various roadways. It's a network of routes and travel paths that allows people to get from one place to another. This is a simple example of a complex network in which the concept of *systems thinking* really does apply.

When I was a kid, our family's summer vacation was always a road trip. The adventure usually started by choosing a new, exciting destination and campgrounds to stay at along the way. We always began with a TripTik from the American Automobile Association (AAA). This map allowed us to plan and plot our entire route. We could start from home and map out each leg of the trip. Because all of us had looked over the maps before we started, we had a clear picture of where we were going, how many days we would stay at each stop, the best way to get to each place, the key attractions to see, the speed traps and construction areas to avoid, and the amount of time that this new journey would take.

While we didn't know it, we had a *systems view*, a map of everything we needed from a state, county, and campground perspective. On many occasions, especially when we made a wrong turn, we pulled out our TripTik to see how to get back on track. We all loved looking at the TripTik each day and finding the arrow that said, "You are here." At every point, we knew exactly where we were with respect to our overall trip, the mileage we had covered, and the distance to our next destination.

Later, when I entered the business world and had to travel the country alone (without the benefit of a TripTik), I often found myself in rental cars trying to read maps, not sure how everything was connected, making the inevitable wrong turns, and getting thoroughly lost with great frequency. This was solved by Hertz and the GPS system called NeverLost. The interesting aspect of this tool was that the more I used it, the less I knew where I was, where I was going, or how I was going to get there. I had abandoned my perception of *travel as a system* and had instead turned my welfare over to the little box on the front seat of the car. On the unfortunate days when my GPS couldn't access the satellites, I was not just lost—I was desperate. I realized that I had no comprehension whatsoever of the big picture of my travel route, the critical parts and pieces of my "system" and how they fit together, and which way to turn to head back in the right direction.

The first time this happened, I had an "aha" moment. I realized what it must feel like to be in an organization that provides no real systems view—where actions are not connected to one another, where the "You are here" sign doesn't include an arrow, and where the linkage of the routes and roads to a final destination doesn't exist.

If you never took a family vacation with a TripTik, never used a GPS, and aren't even sure what AAA is, consider the way Peter Senge describes this feeling in *The Fifth Discipline*. He says that, from childhood, we learn to break down complex problems to make them more manageable. This is initially good, but it leads to another problem. When we do this, says Senge, "we can no longer see the consequences of our actions; we lose our intrinsic sense of connection to a larger whole." At that point, we try to reassemble those pieces mentally, but this often proves futile because the pieces never quite go back as they were meant to. In the end, we give up altogether.

And so, until people can think systemically, they'll never be able to think big. They will not be engaged until they can see the whole system. It's the leaders' responsibility to provide this over-all view.

2. THE IMPACT OF NOT ALLOWING EMPLOYEES TO THINK BIG ABOUT THE OVERALL BUSINESS

Leaders often underestimate the potential of their employees. They don't often appeal to people's highest level of thinking and, as a result, the employees often must operate without the full view of the business.

We once worked with a West Coast pharmaceutical distribution company that was having great difficulty getting people to understand process changes needed to make the business more efficient. In our efforts to integrate a customer-centric view into the order process, we showed them a *Harvard Business Review* article titled "Staple Yourself to an Order." The article described how employees could best understand their customers' service complaints if they actually experienced every step of the product's "journey" from the time an order was placed until final delivery.

To help our client's employees understand the changes in the process *and* the reasons for them, we created a picture of the organization that showed, simply but in great detail, the steps, handoffs, and desired outcomes of fulfilling an order. The leaders wanted to be sure that their people knew the whole process from start to finish.

As one of the leaders watched people work with this newly implemented visual method of communication, he was dumbfounded by the untapped intelligence and energy of many of his employees who interacted with customers on a daily basis. In a moment of insight, he said, "It just occurred to me that we've spent the last 10 years trying to help our people to be as tactically efficient as possible, assuming it would improve the business. But we never told them anything *about* the business! Why did we do this? What if we had focused on the higher issues of the business, like understanding our customers and how to give them what they need? I realize now that we haven't been appealing to the highest level of thinking in our employees. If we had, we would have surely accelerated the improvement of our performance."

The "staple yourself" concept was an inspiration for this company's leadership. It resulted in the recognition that leaders must respect and access the customer care process that resides in the brains of the people who practice it every day. The leaders discovered that most frontline employees did in fact have the ability to comprehend the big picture of the business. As a result, the leaders began to visually portray this big-picture tribal knowledge so that everyone, in every department, could truly understand the entire business. It was transformative.

Here's another example. In the late 1990s, the leaders at Sears were trying to help everyone understand how to create a "compelling place to work, shop, and invest." The CEO sat down beside me at an in-store consulting session to observe some part-time associates talking about the big picture of the retail business and the Sears customer experience. As those conversations started, the CEO began to write down the key issues that the associates apparently didn't understand. Several minutes later, he started crossing out some of those concerns. In another few minutes, he began furiously taking notes on the great ideas that were coming from the part-time associates, who were now enthusiastically discussing how to make Sears a compelling place to work, shop, and invest. He was amazed at the level of interest, literacy, innovation, and the quality of solutions that these part-time associates were coming up with. His comment was, "These ideas are better than the ones I've been getting from my senior team!" It was clear to

> **If leaders appeal to the highest level of thinking in people, they get the highest level of response.**

both of us that if leaders appeal to the highest level of thinking in people, they get the highest level of response.

As we can see from these two examples, if leaders believe in the intelligence of employees and allow them to think about the big picture, employees will be more engaged and will transform the business.

3. THE IMPACT OF NOT THINKING BIG ABOUT BUSINESS PARADOXES

In every strategy, there are components that appear to be in direct conflict, but companies don't always help people make sense of the paradoxes. As a result, people and issues can become polarized.

Recently, a well-known manufacturer had been continually struggling to compete and had not delivered on its operating plan for several years. Its leaders decided to focus on three critical objectives: to reduce inventory in the supply chain, to improve the customer experience, and to increase the number of complete orders shipped on time. The seemingly inconsistent concept of reducing inventory while at the same time increasing the number of complete orders shipped on time confused many employees. The perception was that one day the employees were driven to reduce the amount of inventory in the overall system, and another day they were equally driven to make sure product was on hand to ship to customers as promised. The employees had a problem with what appeared to be corporate doublespeak.

Most of these people didn't understand that both objectives could and should exist simultaneously. Once the paradox was explained, people understood the big picture of the marketplace and how both actions needed to coexist. The result was that the manufacturer performed both tasks and met its annual plan. Ultimately, they reduced their overall working capital by hundreds of millions of dollars and improved customer satisfaction by increasing the number of orders shipped on time.

ANSWERING THE "AND"

Even people who *want* to embrace a strategy can get frustrated trying to understand it. The paradoxes are simply not explored in depth. The key for leaders is to convey the "and" aspect of the strategy and dispel the "or" aspect. Explaining the deepest meaning of the seemingly contradictory nature of the strategy is one of the best cures for the flavor-of-the-month syndrome.

Leaders need to step into the conversations that pit one answer against another. The keys to big-picture thinking are allowing people to have a systems view, making sure that we appeal to their highest level of thinking by showing them the big picture, and reconciling the and-versus-or paradoxes that are at the heart of confusion and mistrust. If people can't see the big picture, they lose their sense of belonging and the ability to see that what they do undoubtedly makes a difference in the business.

QUESTIONS FOR ACTION

1. *Think of your business as a puzzle. What is the puzzle box top that you could send to your people to help them understand the big picture of your business?*

2. *What are the links and connections you need to help people make so they can fully understand how the pieces fit together?*

3. *What are the major systems that your people need to understand and connect with?*

4. *How well defined are these systems?*

5. *What amount of your time is spent exploring how to do a better job instead of how to improve the business?*

6. *Identify the top three paradoxes in play within your organization. In the eyes of your people, are these paradoxes in conflict or in concert?*

8

I Can't Be Engaged If It's Not Mine

W hat do lead paint, asbestos, and PowerPoint presentations have in common? More than you think.

There have been many techniques and approaches that, in their day, appeared to be both commonplace and state-of-the-art. Lead-based paint was touted as the best, cheapest, and longest-lasting protective coating, and we slapped it on everything from houses to toys. In industry, asbestos was once the insulation of choice. As time passed, we realized that not only were these approaches *not* state-of-the-art, but using them was actually detrimental to people's health and well-being.

In the case of lead paint and asbestos, the danger wasn't immediately evident. We kept using them because the consequences took a long time to show up. The same can be said of the PowerPoint presentation. As every businessperson knows, the PowerPoint is the leader's traditional crutch for communicating strategy. To be fair, if it's used as a "bookmark" or "placeholder" to accompany a well-told story, it can be effective. But as it's most commonly used, it can be just as lethal as asbestos and lead paint. In every industry, leaders fire off endless lists of bullet points in an attempt to force-feed company directives. But a PowerPoint simply can't motivate people to challenge their current conclusions, develop new understandings, or think and act differently.

WHAT'S THE POINT OF POWERPOINTS?

If you aren't convinced that static, one-way "information sharing" is toxic as a strategy for mobilizing people, try watching the faces of people in meetings where PowerPoints are used. We've observed hundreds of sessions with anywhere from 30 to 13,000 people trapped in a room, facing a screen with words and graphs projected on it, being dragged to an inevitable, inarguable conclusion that they need to accept. Most leaders are watching the screen, but if they turned around, they'd find a sea of faces in a state of near-terminal boredom. People are simply *waiting for it to be over*. Even the absolute best presentation requires some sort of two-way conversation. How else can people grasp the real meaning of what's being presented?

You can lead a horse to water, but you can't make him "engaged."

Discussion is vital to an individual's commitment and internalization. A cut-and-dried presentation can never do anything more than set the context for what is truly necessary. The tell-and-sell technique may allow us to "check the communication box" for improving performance, but it can't guarantee engagement, commitment, conviction, and the involvement of discretionary effort.

TELL ME, SHOW ME, INVOLVE ME

When was the last time you washed and waxed a rental car? Did you ever go to a store to buy a light bulb when one burned out in your hotel room? Have you ever fixed the roof on your leased apartment? It's painfully obvious that we don't take care of what we don't own. This might be acceptable when it comes to a rental car, a light bulb, or a few shingles, but the real question for business leaders is "What parts of our strategy do our people feel as if they own and want to take care of? And what parts do they feel like they do *not* own?"

You've probably heard this before:

Tell me, and I'll forget.

Show me, and I may remember.

Involve me, and I'll understand.

This wisdom has been attributed to hundreds of sources from Confucius to Anonymous. But in these three short sentences, we find the essence of ownership. And it is ownership that makes the difference in understanding and executing any strategy, and it's involvement and thinking that make the difference in creating ownership.

OWNERSHIP REQUIRES THINKING

One of the most insightful experiences about ownership that we've witnessed involved an employee of a large Canadian bank who was given the opportunity to *actively think* about the business. In a group dialogue, she compared and contrasted major marketplace trends and considered competitive threats, industry consolidation, and consumers' expectations of a more retail-like banking experience.

At the end of the conversation, she said, "This is the first time I've ever learned anything at this bank! You know, learning requires thinking." When we asked her to elaborate, she said, "In 15 years of working here, people have been trying to persuade me to do things differently in order to improve the business. But they never engaged my *thinking* about the business. They just wanted me to buy into the company's perspective and skip all the connections necessary for me to think and then act differently."

Then she hit on the real significance of this episode. "Thinking is a process of boiling down information," she said. "The only way I'll ever change my conclusions is by changing my thinking. When I'm really forced—or invited—to think through what is going on, I can condense a lot of noise into clear conclusions. Now that I've had a chance to actually *think* about our threats and opportunities, I'm beginning to change my ideas about how this bank works and my role in it. And this thinking is demystifying the business for me."

> **"The only way I'll ever change my conclusions is by changing my thinking."**

When leaders invite employees to critically examine the business, they set in motion the thinking that allows employees to own it for themselves.

OWNING A DIFFICULT ISSUE

Here's a notable example of when telling-and-selling and attempts to persuade people to change created just the opposite outcome.

Health-care coverage and the health-care system are among the most difficult areas for any workforce to understand. Even more difficult is to effect any significant change in health-care coverage plans. A large global manufacturer with 22 facilities in North America could no longer carry the cost of employee health care at the same level as in the past. The leaders carefully researched what other companies were doing, how companies were shifting some of the costs, the impact of health-care costs on their ability to compete, the fairness of sharing costs with employees, and the best way to communicate these challenges. They realized the grave importance of their problem when they learned that employees would strike if the health-care issue was not resolved.

To convey the critical points of the new health-care plan, the leaders created a colorful, comprehensive "road show" presentation. They rolled out this show at town hall meetings in every single facility throughout the company in an attempt to educate the entire workforce about what was going to happen and when. After six exhausting weeks, the team returned to headquarters and eagerly took a pulse check of the organization's reaction to the health-care challenge. Here's what they found: All 22 plants had voted to strike. The workers' conclusions were unanimous. "It's not fair" was the general reaction. "It's a one-way edict, and we won't accept it."

The leaders were desperate. They knew they had to do something different. So we worked with this company to carefully create stories that explained the reality of rising health-care costs and connected those realities to the company's ability to compete in the global marketplace. Then, rather than telling the workforce what to think, the leaders presented employees with the same strategic questions that *they* had been trying to address in solving the problem: "If the current health-care-cost trends continue, where will we take the money from so we can remain competitive?" and "What areas of our current health-care plans could we eliminate?" Then, they asked the workforce to discuss in depth the best ways for the company to remain competitive while providing adequate health-care coverage and meeting other stakeholder obligations.

One of these sessions was particularly dramatic. An Ohio manufacturing plant had an especially hostile workforce that was led by a passionate employee representative. This man had lost an arm in an accident at the plant, so he had more reason than most to be concerned about health care and what the company should provide. He began the meeting by suggesting that not only was this a total waste of time, but it was an attempt to brainwash everyone with corporate dictates. After listening to him, many expressed the same opinion. But rather than just walking out, they grudgingly decided to at least go through the motions and cooperate.

And then it happened: After all the critical information and pivotal questions were on the table, the group rigorously discussed all aspects of the situation without being told what to think. At the end of the discussion, most people understood that the health-care approach clearly had to change. Eventually, even the man who had been adamantly opposed to the change joined the discussion—not because it was dictating the answers, but because it was driving the critical questions. In the end, this group of formerly disgruntled workers came up with outstanding recommendations on how to address the health-care problem, and they ultimately reversed the strike vote. And, remarkably, when the process was replicated in the other 21 plants, all of the strike votes were reversed.

> **People will tolerate the conclusions of their leaders, but they will act on their own.**

The principle that struck us like a bolt of lightning was this: "People will tolerate the conclusions of their leaders, but they will act on their own."

The only way to get people to change their conclusions is to engage them in a way that requires them to think and then come to new conclusions for the future. When provided the opportunity to see and examine the same information that leaders can see and examine, and then talk about the same critical questions, good people often come to many of the same conclusions about what needs to be done, even if it's not comfortable for them—like paying more for health care.

THE BUZZ OF OWNERSHIP

Just because you tell your people about something, this doesn't mean that they automatically own it. There's a part they have to do for themselves. When a comedian tells a joke, he sets up the story and delivers the punch line. But before you can laugh, you have to make the connection between the story, the punch line, and your ability to relate to it. If those connections aren't there—*if you don't make them yourself*—the joke's not funny. It's only an "aha" if *you* add the crucial part.

When we try to communicate through projected graphs and fancy words, we end up baffled when people don't leap to their feet in a standing ovation when the PowerPoint is done. We need to recognize that it's not the on-screen, multicolored presentation with rock music pounding in the background that motivates people. It's the gentle but careful orchestration of the ahas of understanding that inspires people to want to go out and change something about themselves, their teams, their behaviors, and their outcomes. You can't *tell* an aha—you have to create the conditions for someone else to discover it. And when you do, it spreads like wildfire, and you're passionate to tell someone else so that they can have the same experience.

So gaining commitment from people—motivating them to believe in your business and to want to give it all they have— requires leaders to set up the right environment for the aha moments. Until we overcome our dependency on PowerPoints and other tell-and-sell methods, we'll never understand the importance of allowing our people to think and learn on their own. Only when they do the work and feel the sense of accomplishment will they embrace new insights, tackle new commitments, and reach new conclusions.

QUESTIONS FOR ACTION

1. *Would your people say that you're using PowerPoints effectively to tell a story, or that it's a one-way presentation that's as lethal as asbestos when it comes to engaging them?*

2. *On a scale of 1 to 10, how would you rate yourself at involving your people in thinking through the most critical questions of your business? What can you do to change?*

3. *Would you be a tell-me, show-me, or involve-me practitioner?*

4. *Consider the statement "People will tolerate the conclusions of their leaders but act on their own." How could you test the validity of this statement with your employees to determine if it's true?*

5. *How are you creating the environment for your people to experience for themselves the aha moments that are vital for their engagement?*

9

I Can't Be Engaged If My Leaders Don't Face Reality

L et's get real about engaging people to execute strategy. While executives passionately formulate strategy and call for the transformation of their companies, the reality is that most strategies are hopelessly stuck on the drawing boards where they were created. Why is this? How can we solve this problem?

WHAT WE'RE DOING IS NOT WORKING

We've refined our strategic objectives, debated our critical success factors, nuanced our balanced scorecards, and rallied the troops at our annual conferences. And to top it off, we've captured all this wisdom in some great PowerPoint decks that we pass around for days, weeks, and months—long after the conference's slogan, "We Are One," fades away. We've done all that we should, but our best-laid plans are not delivering. Something is not working. Why? Let's begin with what the researchers and experts tell us.

The authors of the well-respected book *The Balanced Scorecard*, Robert S. Kaplan and David P. Norton, tell us that barely 10 percent of all strategies are actually implemented. From Ernst & Young, we know that in terms of actually delivering results, strategy *execution* is more important than strategy *creation*. Zoghi analysts report that at least 70 percent of all change initiatives fail due to things related to people, not market forces. These include the inability to lead, lack of teamwork, unwillingness to take initiative, and inability to deal with change. And from Gallup, we've learned that nearly three-quarters of employees today don't consider themselves "actively engaged" in their work. This translates to a cost of nearly $300 billion a year in lost productivity in the United States alone. Those are pretty sobering statistics.

OUR REALITY IS A CANYON

In most organizations today, the reality is that there are huge gaps among three groups of people: the leaders, who can see what needs to be done but don't have their hands on the levers of change; the doers, who have their hands on the levers of change but simply can't see the big picture; and managers, who are hopelessly caught in the middle. Leaders say things like, "This is our vision and mission." Doers say, "Sounds blue sky to me. What does it mean for me and my people?" Leaders say, "You need to work smarter!" and doers counter with, "We can't possibly work any harder!" Leaders exclaim, "You are empowered!" and doers respond, "More of that flavor-of-the-month management." Meanwhile, managers sit in the middle of this conversation trying to figure out which side they're on and whether they should be sending clearer messages to their workers or listening better so they can understand their leaders. Managers often feel as if they are standing on a narrow, crumbling precipice in the center of the action.

"The Canyon" (on the facing page, also shown in color at the center of the book) captures this conversation and how people experience this reality every day. Take a look.

In the illustration, there are three main levels, each separated by a canyon. Upon closer examination, you'll see leaders putting together all of the pieces of the strategic puzzle while keeping an eye to the future. At the same time, they just can't figure out how to get managers and doers to execute on their fresh new strategies. As a result, they feel as if the rest of the organization just doesn't get it.

Next, managers balance on a narrow strip between the leaders and doers. They have been thrust into a role where they are being torn between what the leaders *want* them to do and what the doers *need* them to do. They are asked to take the greatest risk and execute the most significant change, and they've been given the least support in playing their part.

Then we see the doers, deep in the trenches, frustrated because they're overwhelmed as they bail water out of a cubicle that is constantly refilling. They are so focused on what they must do in the next five minutes that it's impossible to think bigger about the business. They can't see beyond the work that keeps caving in on them. Many of them want to crawl out of the trenches and scream, "I'm not going to take this anymore!" For now, they just do what they are told and are careful not to raise their heads above the trench.

The reality of every business is a canyon.

In the midst of all this chaos, the external winds of change continue to whip across the entire scene. The organization seems utterly unable to align its people, resources, and actions to create better business results today, let alone tomorrow.

As a side act in the lower right corner, the poor customers are wondering why they're not written into this story, why nobody's focused on them, and what they have to do to get some service. Eventually, they'll go to another company where they will get the attention they demand.

The image of the canyon reflects reality as it's often described by people at all levels of an organization. It's a tangible representation that has visually captured the frustration and reality of many people. Defining and addressing reality is the first step toward creating engaged employees who are ready to execute the strategy. Unfortunately, many leaders today don't face up to this reality, and their employees and organizations suffer.

GETTING PAST FINGER-POINTING

The picture of the canyon can kick-start conversations that most organizations and the people in them *have never known how to have before*. When we've used this picture with hundreds of businesses around the world, we nearly always hear, "That's us!"

No one realizes that the canyon is a *natural* state, the result of the acceleration of changes that originate in the marketplace.

The most common first reaction is for each level to point fingers at the others as the reason why strategies aren't working. The blame game reigns supreme because no one realizes that the canyon is a *natural* state, the result of the acceleration of changes that originate in the marketplace. Once we see the tornado of the changing marketplace next to the challenges of leaders, managers, and doers, we can begin to understand that the creation, deployment, engagement, and execution of strategy form a process that involves all three levels.

The next reaction from people in most organizations is to ask, "What's the root cause?" This is when the finger-pointing usually stops, and people begin to realize that not everyone is on the same level, and therefore can't see the same things, and no one is actively working to build the bridges that can connect the vision, actions, and outcomes. As one company executive said, "Until we put Humpty Dumpty back together, we'll never be able to deliver on our aspirations for the future."

A key aspect of the art of engagement is the ability and willingness to visualize reality, so that once you have looked at it you won't dismiss it or slide it into a drawer. The canyon screams back that these are our issues and we must decide what we're going to do about them. The canyon can't be as easily ignored as a PowerPoint, a speech, or a gap analysis. It represents a powerful mirror of reality. It's a call to action to understand and address those things that divide us. Real connection requires a new accountability, one that acknowledges that everyone plays a role in the rampant disengagement of the organization.

WHAT SIZE IS YOUR CANYON?

When viewing the canyon as a way to assess their own current reality, business leaders often ask many of the same questions. These questions are aimed at assessing "What size is our canyon?" Combining the visual sketch with specific questions has enabled many organizations to talk about issues that they didn't know how to talk about, the very issues that were significant impediments to engaging their people to execute strategy. So, if you want to find out what your canyon looks like, there are some questions that can help you determine how to do that.

Start by looking at the color version of this canyon at the center of this book. (You can also go to www.rootsofengagement.com

to download a copy to use with your team.) Look at all the imagery on the canyon visual and explore the following questions. They can be answered for the entire organization or any intact work team. This is a good experience for an individual, but it's even more powerful with a group of 6 to 10.

1. What do you see overall?
2. Look at the tornado. Which of these forces do you think are having the greatest impact?
3. What do you think leaders see?
4. What do you think managers see?
5. What do you think doers see?
6. Do they see the same thing? Why or why not?
7. Are there canyons that exist within any of the three groups we've just discussed? What are they?
8. Have the canyons always existed?
9. What are the root causes?
10. Who's to blame?
11. Look again at the tornado. Which specific forces would you add? How are these forces impacting the company?
12. Consider all the images in the canyon. Which ones most resonate for this organization or team? Why?
13. What images would you add to the canyon that capture even more precisely the truth of this current reality?
14. What other quotes would you add that you've heard or even said about the organization or team?
15. Of all the images or quotes on the canyon, which one or two are the most real or relevant to you personally?
16. How have you contributed to these?
17. As an organization or team, where are the most significant canyons?
18. What can we do to build bridges over these canyons?
19. If we were to redraw this picture after we've bridged the canyons, what should it look like?

20. What are the most important actions we can take to begin to address these canyons and redraw the picture?

Even when it's acknowledged, the canyon is often misinterpreted by many people as a criticism of "what we've always done." Only when people can see that the source of the canyon is the external marketplace and that the need to change is *not an indictment of their past performance* will they openly embrace the reality of the

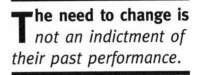

The need to change is *not an indictment of their past performance.*

canyon. The way to begin doing that is by truthfully answering the question "What size is your canyon?" and then deciding what you're willing to do about it.

QUESTIONS FOR ACTION

1. *From various sources, we know that most strategies are not executed and the majority of people in companies are not engaged. What are your engagement statistics? Do you know what they are? How could you find out? What does your canyon look like?*

2. *Consider your answer to question 1. How could you estimate the amount of money that lack of engagement is costing your company? How much are you leaving on the table by not tackling your canyon issues that are holding back engagement and execution?*

3. *What could you do to build the understanding that the canyon is a natural state driven by marketplace changes rather than creating the impression that someone has "screwed up" and "we're dysfunctional"?*

4. *How well do you think your organization or team recognizes that the canyon is a natural state? How could this recognition accelerate your organization's actions to bridge the canyon?*

The Six Keys to Engagement

*L*et's recap the major reasons why people aren't engaged in strategy execution. We've learned that people can't be engaged if they're overwhelmed with work, if the strategy is not relevant to them, if they don't feel safe in learning new skills and behaviors, if they don't understand the big picture, if they are just told what to think, and if their leaders refuse to embrace reality. All of these are responsible for carving out deeper canyons between people and their organizations and contribute to the sobering statistics on disengagement and nonexecution.

But there are ways to stop the madness! In Part 3, we'll explore the six keys to artfully engaging people and overcoming these barriers. These include keeping people connected to organizations through images and stories, creating pictures together that liberate their imaginations about the business, and helping them to believe in their leaders and managers, as well as inviting people to own and solve their business problems, to play the entire game of the business, and to practice before they take on new strategic challenges.

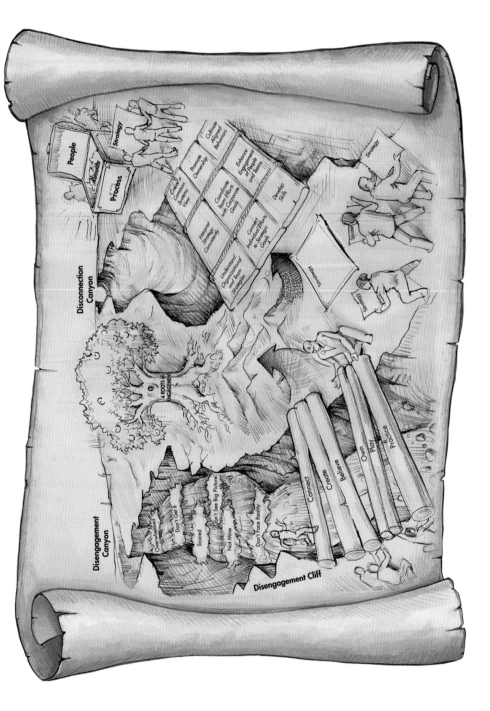

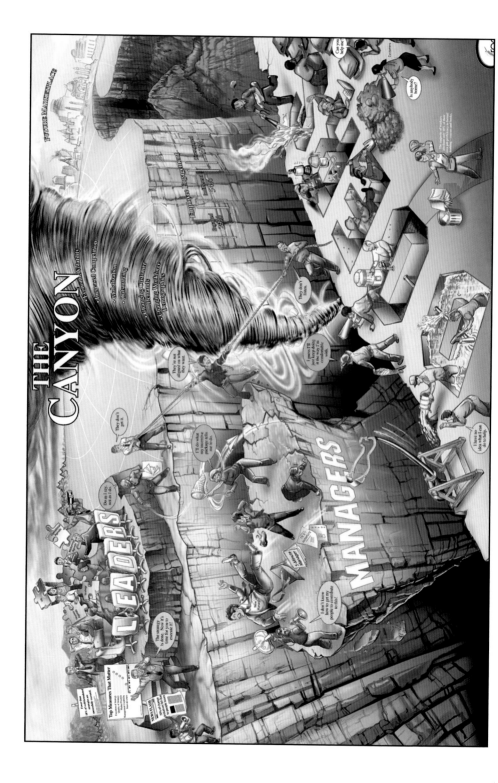

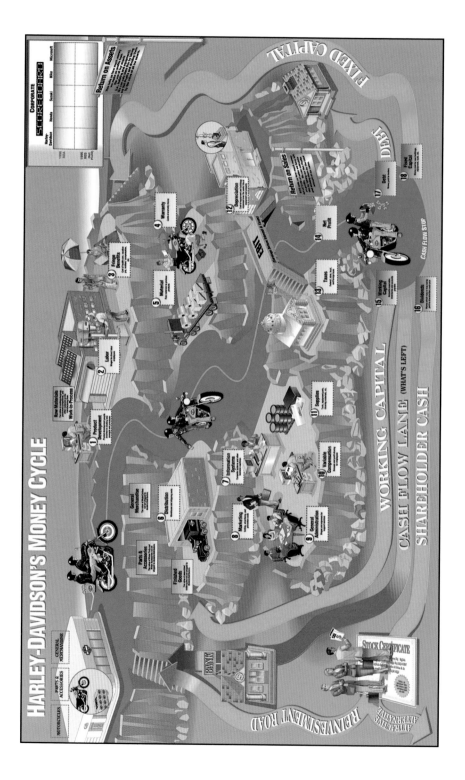

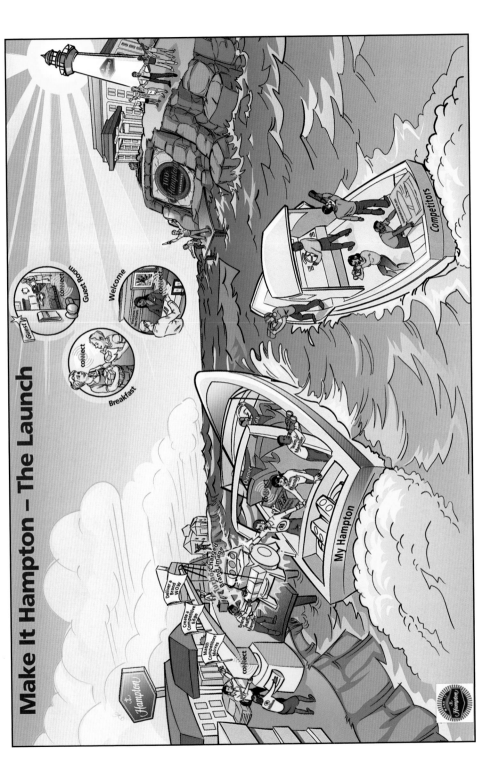

BRIDGING THE CANYON

LEADERS

MANAGERS

INDIVIDUAL CONTRIBUTORS

DEVELOP CAPABILITIES

Cultivate Aligned Behaviors

Promote Ownership

Enhance Engagement of People and Teams

Develop Skills

CONNECT GOALS

Coordinate Team Efforts with Corporate Goals

Connect Individual Efforts to Strategic Goals

CREATE LINE OF SIGHT

Create a Common Systems View

Interpret Strategy Consistently

Understand Organizational and Team Strategies

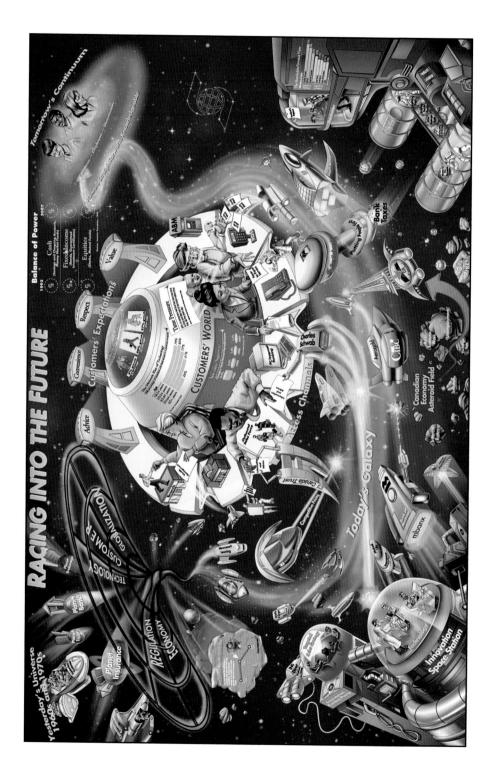

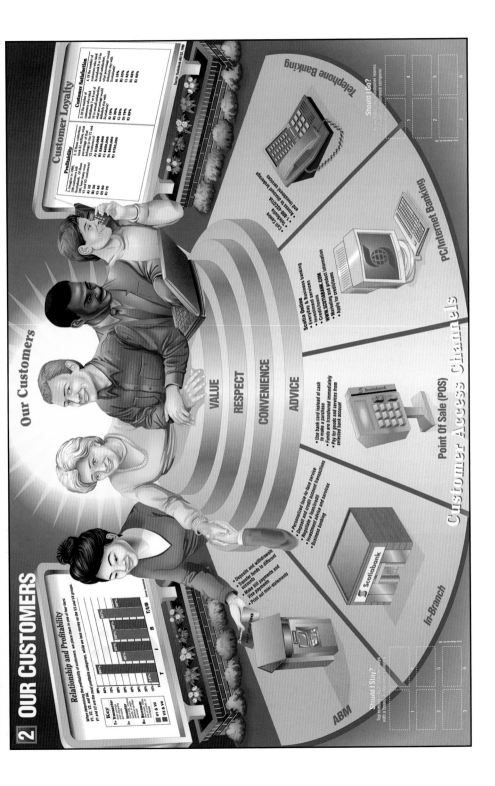

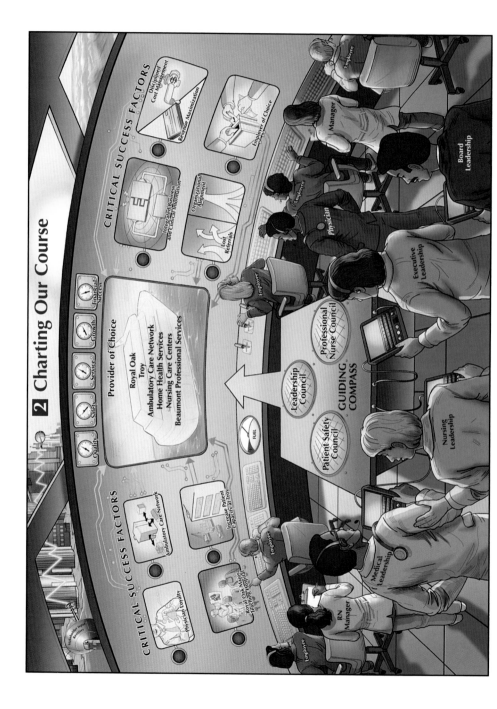

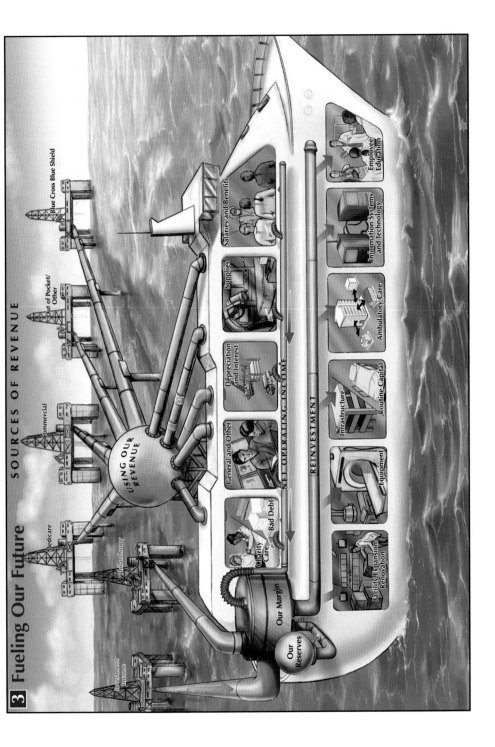

3 Fueling Our Future

SOURCES OF REVENUE

Blue Cross Blue Shield
Out of Pocket/Other
Commercial
Medicare
Philanthropy
Investment Income

USING OUR REVENUE

Charity Care
Bad Debt
General and Other
Depreciation and Interest
Supplies
Salaries and Benefits

NET OPERATING INCOME

REINVESTMENT

Facility Expansion Renovation
Equipment
Infrastructure
Routine Capital
Ambulatory Care
Information Systems and Technology
Employee Education

Our Margin
Our Reserves

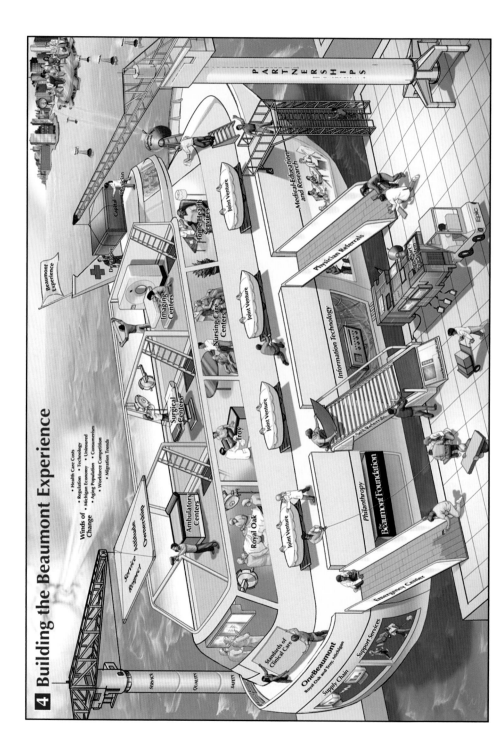

4 Building the Beaumont Experience

Key #1: Connecting through Images and Stories

It's impossible to think without pictures. If I said to you, "Don't think of a pink elephant," your mind would refuse to obey. Go ahead, try not to think of a pink elephant. Or try this. Imagine an area that's 57,600 square feet. Got it? Maybe, maybe not. But if I'd said, "Imagine a space the size of a football field, including the end zones," you'd probably know just what I

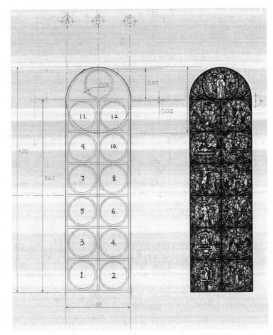

Visual storytelling in the beauty of a stained glass window.

mean. People connect through images and stories, not just cold, bare words.

Humans think visually. Throughout history, pictures have told stories that draw people into the world around them. In the Middle Ages, stained glass windows helped people understand the religious and classical stories that were important in their lives. The windows of Chartres Cathedral in France tell biblical stories in a series of sequential pictorials. The picture on the previous page shows a window such as this—one in which the panels turn a decorative window into an educational experience. If you follow the accompanying "blueprint," you can see how the story flows from bottom to top.

By the time of the Renaissance, more realistic paintings intensified the connection between stories and people. Two centuries later, Baroque artists made the stories even more contemporary, with classical figures wearing "modern" clothes in "modern" settings. Each successive artist attempted to make stories more practical and real for the people of their time. And they all knew that spoken or written communication could convey data, but visual storytelling was a powerful way to influence people.

VISUAL STORYTELLING IN BUSINESS

Every business has stories to tell. Organizations can take a cue from the artists of the Middle Ages by visualizing stories that help people make sense of their business. In *The Leader's Guide to Storytelling*, author Stephen Denning says: "At a time when corporate survival requires transformative change, leadership involves getting people to act in unfamiliar and unwelcome ways. Analysis may excite the mind, but it hardly offers a route to the heart. Stories can translate dry and abstract numbers into compelling pictures."

> **Visual storytelling accelerates understanding and forms a fast, consistent, common language for engagement.**

If the best way to communicate meaning is with a story, then the best way to tell an engaging, memorable story is with a picture. Visual storytelling accelerates understanding and forms a fast, consistent, common language for engagement.

ACCELERATING UNDERSTANDING

Let's demonstrate how visualization affects simplicity, speed, and clarity. Read this description and guess who it is *before you turn the page*: This person, a well-known 20th century American, has a high forehead, a strong nose, and a dimple in the center of the chin. There is a calm yet piercing quality about the eyes. The eyebrows are not arched, but follow the curve of the eyes. Perhaps the most memorable feature is the light hair, swept back from the face, thick and curly, cut just below the ears.

Do you know who this is? Okay, turn the page.

How did you do? How long did it take you to formulate an answer from the description? Then, how long did it take you to understand it when you saw the picture? If you're like everyone else, the difference is stunning. In many cases, it's about 40 seconds versus 4—a 10-fold difference in speed.

What is it about a description that the picture shortcuts? First, you can see the whole thing. The picture puts the pieces together, so you don't have to imagine how to connect them into a system—in this case, the system is the face of Albert Einstein. Because Einstein was such a well-known celebrity, the picture instantly connects to something we can associate with. Every component of the written description is open to a wide range of interpretation, based on your assumptions. But the *picture* leaves little room for misinterpretation and quickly conveys the exact meaning in a brief moment.

So what does all this have to do with business? When people think about a system visually, they can associate it with things they already know. And when we use visualization to portray the operations of a business, employees can more easily understand difficult concepts. Images eliminate the opportunity for widespread misinterpretation and thus generate a common, quickly understood language.

VISUALIZATION AS A LANGUAGE

A language is a way of exchanging ideas or feelings by using words, signs, or symbols with common meanings. The language of visualization is more versatile than the written or spoken word because it can concisely carry the meaning of either a few ideas or a larger number of messages.

There are many methods that are used in business to help both employees and customers think about and recognize the important concepts that a company needs to communicate. The chart on the next page presents some of the visualization techniques that are applied in business. Root Learning conceptual artist Victor Zhang created the Pyramid of Visualization, which starts with simple imagery and progresses to more complex techniques. Each of these levels of visualization can help illustrate the stories of any business.

The simplest of these techniques is *visual notes*, which we use whenever we draw arrows and circles to help us remember infor-

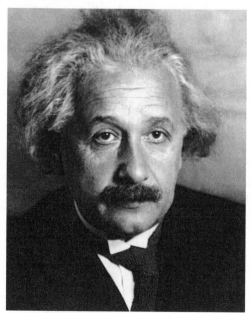

Albert Einstein.

Corbis

mation. Visual notes help us understand the relationship between pieces so we can better grasp the whole. The next level is *icons*, universal symbols that help us navigate through life without using words. With icons, understanding is quick and requires no questions; people know exactly what is being conveyed by a single image. The third level, *drawings* or *photos*,

The Pyramid of Visualization

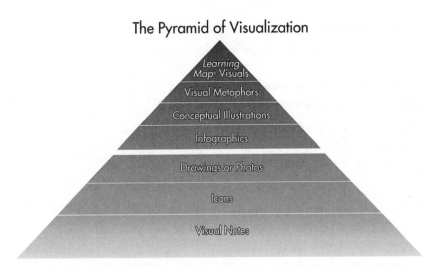

Learning Map® Visuals

Visual Metaphors

Conceptual Illustrations

Infographics

Drawings or Photos

Icons

Visual Notes

can convey a brief story without the need for reading. These go beyond visual notes and icons because they capture motion and enable detailed recall. The fourth level, *infographics*, is familiar to anyone who has seen an issue of *USA Today*. Basic graphics and facts can be combined to form a picture that makes sense at a glance.

The top three steps of the pyramid have the potential to be the most helpful in engaging people in stories of their business, so we'll explore these in a bit more detail.

CONCEPTUAL ILLUSTRATIONS

This entails more than a single image; it's the visualization of a system with several components. A mural that tells a story through a series of images is a good example. Another example is a visual timeline that describes a business yesterday and today and projects forward into tomorrow.

One of the best applications for conceptual visualization is helping people understand business systems. Once systems are visualized, people can grasp the big idea, including the steps, the inputs, the handoffs, and how each step contributes to delivering the greatest overall value.

For example, in hopes of getting customers to make return visits, many retailers encourage employees to engage customers by improving the service experience. Banners are hung, advertising taglines are developed, and contests are launched to motivate employees to continually exceed customer expectations. Here's the

> **O**nce systems are visualized, people can grasp the big idea.

challenge: because all of the employees are involved with different parts of the system, they never comprehend exactly what the company is trying to create for the customer.

The sketch below is a conceptual illustration of a Banana Republic retail store. Taking the roof off the store and visualizing

"Taking off the roof" shows the customer journey.

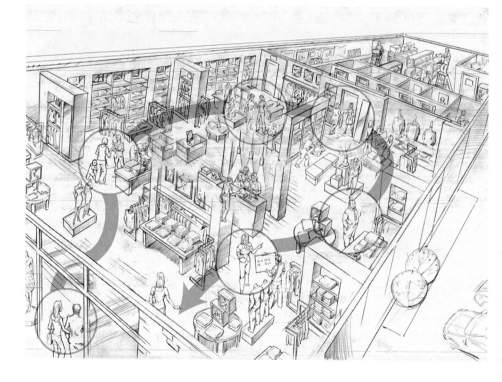

the entire customer engagement experience as a system allows us to see the customers' journey from the moment they decide to enter the store until long after they leave. It's difficult to see all this without a visual. When employees can use this conceptual illustration to view the experience from above, they understand how each step connects to the next one, and how each employee contributes to the full experience. By illustrating a systems view, we create a perspective that frontline employees rarely see, yet is necessary to create a satisfying customer experience.

VISUAL METAPHORS

Metaphors allow us to simplify new or complex information by comparing it with something we already know. Metaphors do graphically what zip files do for data management on a computer: they "shrinkwrap" large amounts of information into manageable, usable formats.

Aristotle said, "The soul never thinks without a picture," and many people have said, "A picture is worth a thousand words." We could go on to say, "If a picture is worth a thousand words, a metaphor is worth a thousand pictures." However, according to Zhang, "The real magic of using metaphors in business is that *they create a visual language where one does not exist.*" As this visual language is created, it gives people at all levels of an organization a way to exchange data, share information, and discuss the business so they can drive performance.

> "The real magic of using metaphors in business is that *they create a visual language where one does not exist.*"

Consider this example. The drawing on the next page is a metaphorical picture of the changing cable marketplace. For anyone who views this picture, the metaphor creates a visual language about the need to change.

A picture shows who has the real power.

The consumer is shown as a "superman" who is clearly in control of the scene. He has many options of where to plug in and select the service provider he prefers. The competitors are all vying for his business, and the consumer will determine the winners and losers. This picture shows the current state of the marketplace and four major storylines wrapped into one metaphor—(1) excess capacity, (2) customer is king, (3) intense competition, and (4) the power shift from providers to cable users. The metaphor emotionally draws people into the reality that not everyone will survive in the emerging marketplace.

The obvious strength of visual metaphor is that it's simple, it's fast, and it consolidates a wealth of information into one clear, understandable picture. But its true power is the emotional connection it creates with people about the "life-and-death" struggles playing out within the industry and the organization. It becomes obvious that if we continue to do what we've done in the past, we do so at our own peril. This is a powerful way to engage people to effect change in an organization.

LEARNING MAP® VISUALS

At the top of the pyramid, the *Learning Map®* visual incorporates many of the steps into one picture by using icons, infographics, drawings, conceptual illustration, and metaphors. In this way, companies with 70 to 700,000 people can create an understanding about how their business works and how each person contributes to making it better. These visuals not only convey large amounts of information but also expose people to the drama, emotion, and complex stories in their businesses.

Learning Map® visuals are important for creating an environment of engagement because they assemble the stories and pictures of a business into one, clear, understandable mosaic. We'll take an inside look at the *Learning Map®* experience in an upcoming chapter.

THE POWER OF VISUALIZATION IN BUSINESS

Visualization is a critical ingredient of engagement with many benefits:

1. Visualization makes it easy to think in systems. It allows people to understand, connect, and focus systemically.
2. Visualization creates simplicity. It forces us to "think simpler." You can't draw a crisp picture of something that hasn't been thought through in great detail.
3. Visualization captures the drama of the business. It illustrates struggles, risks, threats, opportunities, and emotion in ways that data and words cannot. Tapping into this emotion challenges complacency and inspires activism within a business.
4. Visualization enables us to think big or think strategically by showing us the whole. Thinking big allows us to focus on the major forces that drive our business rather than the everyday tactics that often occupy much of our time.
5. Visualization appeals to most learners. In general, a visual culture is quickly replacing the traditional print culture, and

there's no question that it will be the approach of choice for the future.

6. Visualization provides for quick recall. Visual images help most people retain information efficiently.

7. Visualization enables nonlinear connections. Not everybody learns in a straight, progressive path. Each of us has to personalize the connections.

8. Visualization acts as a universal common language by minimizing misinterpretations. It's a consistent way to communicate among different cultures and languages.

9. Visualization allows visual storytelling. It enables people to easily see an integrated story and talk about how they can add to it.

10. Visualization connects people because it can display both facts and emotion. It conveys not only how the business looks but also how it feels.

In the first part of this book, we saw that there are many inhibitors to engagement. Some of these are complexity, lack of relevance, the inability to think big or in systems, and the absence of ownership. Visualization is a powerful language of engagement that counteracts many of these inhibitors. To engage the human spirit, leaders must connect employees to the struggle, passion, and emotion of the business. In so doing, leaders will ignite their employees' creative ability and skills.

QUESTIONS FOR ACTION

1. *Every business has stories to tell. What are the strategic business stories that could add meaning to your lifeless facts and figures?*

2. *Consider all the business systems you interact with. Which system is least understood? How could a picture of that system help everyone to understand how it works?*

3. *What metaphor best describes your overall marketplace? How would a visual representation—or at least just a visual description—of this metaphor engage your people in the emotion and drama of your business?*

4. *Consider a strategy, initiative, or just an objective that is not crisply understood by the people in your business. What is it? Could a story or images drive clarity?*

11

Key #2: Creating Pictures Together

H ave you ever been in a restaurant or bar and asked the waiter
for a pen and an extra paper napkin? Why did you do that?
You might have had a flash of inspiration, an idea that you wanted
to capture first for yourself, and then show to someone else. But
why did you have to draw it on a napkin?

Here's why napkin sketching may have worked for you. First,
it allowed you to get all your ideas down so that you could take a

You don't need to be an artist to sketch an idea.

step back and see if they made sense. When you did this, you most likely asked for another napkin and drew version 2.0. Then, you looked at your second sketch to be sure it included all the key parts of your insight. You drew some arrows and connected stick figures to show how it all fit together. Then you called your waiter back to ask for yet another napkin.

By this time, you may have considered what to emphasize. So on the third napkin, you made some of the lines stronger and some of the arrows bigger than others. Version 3.0 was complete! When you left the bar, you took the napkin with you. You were excited about showing it to a few colleagues to discuss just how big the idea really was.

Once your colleagues reviewed your refined napkin sketch, you listened to their ideas and redrew it once more, adding the elements that they said were missing. You created version 4.0. This version could be traced back to your original sketch, but its latest rendition seemed far more exciting.

If napkin sketching can achieve that kind of engagement on a piece of tissue, imagine what could happen if business teams drew group napkin sketches that could rapidly evolve their best thinking. This is called *visual iteration,* and it's a process by which people combine their ideas into a rapid succession of images that evoke common meaning and ownership. Visually iterated sketches and dialogue can quickly liberate and connect the best thinking of individuals in a way that causes people to say, "Wow! We could never have created that by ourselves!"

> **W**hat could happen if business teams drew group napkin sketches that could rapidly evolve their best thinking?

This approach can be used to address a major business problem, formulate a new strategy, frame a process redesign, or detail an execution plan.

ARE YOU THINKING WHAT I'M THINKING?

"I'll know it when I see it" is what many people say when they have strong opinions that they can't easily express. This suggests that they're searching for a way to explain what they intuitively know but can't readily describe or articulate. This inability to share what we're really thinking can be a temporary annoyance when choosing new carpeting, but it can have profound ramifications when it comes to being on the same page in terms of business strategy.

Here's an example of the magnitude and opportunity of this challenge. A $30 billion chemical company was trying to visualize its strategy. The third sketch in a series of iterations immediately resonated with the chairman, who exclaimed, "That's exactly it! *That's* what I've been trying to explain to everyone! It captures precisely what we need to accomplish in the years ahead." The vice chairman looked worried as he said, "Is that how you see what we're trying to achieve?" When the chairman gave an enthusiastic "Yes!" the vice chairman replied, "Well then, we'd better talk, because that's not what I thought you meant—and that's clearly not what I've been doing." In an instant, the power of visual iteration to align thinking became very clear.

THINKING TOGETHER IN PICTURES

Here's what caused that power: When visual iteration and dialogue are combined, they elicit people's opinions, beliefs, attitudes, and conclusions. Then, those thoughts can be publicly challenged and the picture can be redrawn so that it eventually means the same thing to everyone who's been part of its creation. In almost all cases, this "drawing out and drawing in" results in a final image that causes a group to stand back and look at it in awe. The awe comes from the depth, clarity, drama, and energy that the sketch has captured. In the words of more than one team, "That's magical!"

So what's the magic in visual iteration? It's that a team of people searching for a solution starts in one place and finishes in an entirely different place. Let's look at another example.

The sketches below illustrate how senior leaders of General Motors described the global marketplace. It was vital for everyone to view the urgency of the marketplace in the same way. The leaders started with a simple sketch of how they saw the external environment. As the quality of the thinking improved with each iteration, so did the ability to add greater depth and meaning to the sketch. In the end, the challenges of the global marketplace became clear, and the final picture was distributed worldwide as a way for the many employees of General Motors to think about the competitive marketplace and prepare their strategic responses.

General Motors' visual iterations.

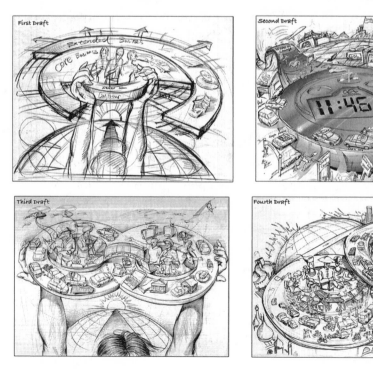

Here's another example. The leaders at Pepsi were looking to create a case for change. They wanted to help employees in North America understand how different their business was becoming. Yet embracing these differences would require the roles of almost all employees to change significantly. Delivery drivers' tasks were going to evolve from just delivering products to merchandising and advising customers on new offerings. And production forecasters would need to do a much better job of anticipating demand for the many new beverage products Pepsi would be introducing into the market.

As with most companies, initial attempts to communicate these changes met with strong resistance. Pepsi leaders needed a way to communicate the business dynamics of their marketplace to their employees so that they would understand *why* so many strategic changes were being made. Each time the marketplace was visually drawn (a napkin sketch), it surfaced key questions for the leaders to think about so that the illustration captured what was most important. The process, in fact, became a great way to facilitate strategic thinking and decision-making for the team. Each iteration brought greater depth and simplicity to the picture.

These sketches are shown on the following page. The first sketch attempted to frame the fundamental idea that "Beverage Street," Pepsi's business landscape, was changing very rapidly. As the team further explored the forces of change, the second visual iteration introduced the actual customer channels of the business as the storefronts on the street, with each depicting what they were asking for from Pepsi. The mileposts down the center of the street highlighted powerful consumer dynamics, such as that aging baby boomers were developing new demands and expectations for their beverage choices. The third sketch built further on these concepts, showing that all of these influences were culminating in dramatic changes to consumers' beverage preferences and buying habits—thus, the case for change.

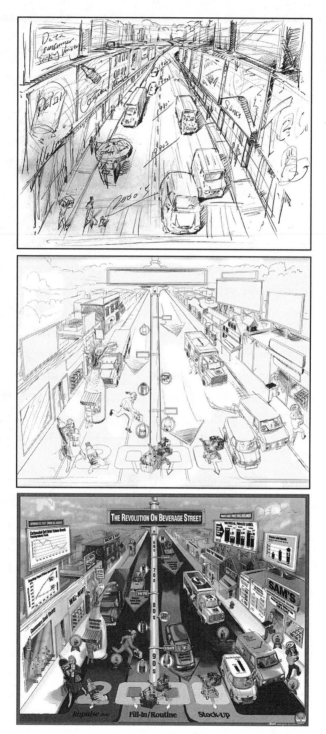

Pepsi's visual iterations.

With each iteration, the multiple driving forces of the business continued to be more seamlessly integrated into the overall picture. The completed version can also be found in Chapter 14, with more detail on exactly how it was used to launch Pepsi's total beverage strategy. Pepsi's CEO said, "Somehow, we've been able to shrink, highlight, and integrate 400 pages of strategic plans into a medium that most of our people can understand. I'm still not sure how we did it."

Simply said, visual iteration is using sequential pictures to help build ownership and establish precise meaning. It is this absence of precision that prevents people from thinking together and delivering performances that they're very capable of.

An executive at a national restaurant chain accomplished this on his own, without the aid of a gifted artist to draw visual iterations. The chain had become obsessed with improving the cleanliness of its restaurants. Despite memos, incentive plan changes, and inspections by senior leaders, cleanliness in the eyes of customers still wasn't improving. The executive (who had experienced visual iteration with another project) knew that he needed to establish a precise, clear meaning of what "cleanliness" meant in their restaurants, and he figured out how to engage in visual iteration without an artist's help.

He asked the managers of 40 restaurants to take a photo of what they thought "restaurant cleanliness" looked like and bring the picture to the next area meeting. As they arrived, each manager taped a 4-by-6-inch photo on a designated wall of the conference room. Even before the meeting started, the problem—and the solution—was obvious. Each restaurant had a different idea of what cleanliness looked like. The executive said, "If cleanliness doesn't mean the same thing to each of us, we'll have no chance of creating it consistently for our customers." As a group, the managers chose the one picture that best represented the cleanliness standard that they wanted to achieve and used it as a model for improving performance on this important customer priority.

WHAT HAPPENS WHEN TEAMS USE VISUAL ITERATION?

As we can see, visual iteration offers clear advantages to teams as they work to build clarity, alignment, ownership, and understanding. However, five distinct benefits stand out and can be significant catalysts for accelerating strategy execution.

1. VISUAL ITERATION ALLOWS PEOPLE TO SEE THEIR IDEAS ON PAPER IN ORDER TO MAKE SURE THAT THEY'RE WELL THOUGHT THROUGH AND CONVEY WHAT THEY INTEND TO CONVEY. Like a mirror, the image should reflect what a team says. Then, it will allow them to question whether what they *said* is really what they *meant*.

Visual iteration sets ideas in motion. It helps people see the quality and connections of their thoughts and ideas and then evaluate their completeness. Often, only through visual iteration can people realize that many of their ideas aren't "finished" or completely thought through.

As strange as it sounds, many teams aren't exactly sure what they mean by the concept of engaging their people, or exactly what they want to achieve from doing it. We've worked with team after team whose members have been very clear about what something is *not* but only vaguely certain about what that same thing *is*. Strategies, business plans, and initiatives have large gaps between familiar words that are used to describe them and the exact details of what needs to be done differently. It's only when we test the accuracy of the words by trying to visualize them that we realize how little is nailed down.

> **W**hen leaders try to create a picture of their strategy, they discover that it's impossible to visualize fuzz. Visual iteration forces fuzz into focus.

Often when leaders try to create a picture of their strategy, they discover that it's impossible to visualize fuzz. "Fuzz" isn't dryer lint. It's made up of incomplete intentions, half-thought-through themes, and unclear outcomes. Interestingly, fuzz is prominent in most organizations as leaders try to engage people to execute strategy. Visual iteration forces fuzz into focus.

2. VISUAL ITERATION ENABLES PEOPLE TO THINK IN SYSTEMS. Visual iteration ensures that leaders have considered the whole issue, not just a piece of it. Successive sketches have an amazing ability to actually change the way people look at an idea or concept. And when people change how they look at a concept, they begin to change their thinking about what the concept means.

The simplest example is the old fable about the blind men and the elephant. One man touches the elephant's tusk and believes that the elephant is a spear. Another touches the trunk and says it's a snake. A third man touches the elephant's tail and thinks it's a rope. And so on. All of them come to the wrong conclusion because they can't see the whole elephant.

When we touch just a part of a system, we conclude that it is the whole system.

The same problem exists when people can't think in terms of systems. Because they touch only a piece of the system, they conclude that it *is* the whole system. For example, when a company decides to convert to integrated supply chain management across several divisions, the first reaction of the employees in some of the divisions is usually, "This won't work for us." Each division has a limited ability to conceptualize the greater benefit of the supply chain system for everyone, so their immediate conclusion is that they've lost control. Only when they can "visualize big" can they see the incompleteness of their conclusion.

3. VISUAL ITERATION HELPS PEOPLE TO ABANDON THEIR OWN PICTURES AND EMBRACE BETTER, CO-CREATED PICTURES. The visual iteration process leads to ownership because people create a new picture *together*. Whenever people attempt to engage each other on strategy, initiatives, or actions—whether it's a team of safety engineers or the senior executives of a Fortune 500 company—almost inevitably, the same thing happens. Each person starts with a mental picture of what they believe the group should do. That picture is built on what the person individually thinks is the best course of action. This perspective is reinforced by their own experiences, attitudes, and conclusions. Unfortunately, in this situation we all tend to hide our own mental picture under the proverbial table and begin to lobby, consciously or unconsciously, for our picture to be chosen. This is a natural human tendency—we *like* our ideas and we want everyone else to like them too. The bigger the ego, the stronger the lobbying. We want to win!

But an interesting thing happens with the introduction of visual iteration. When everyone has a chance to literally put their pictures on the table and integrate them into one combined image of the best ideas in the room, people stop lobbying and start seeing their own ideas in the picture. The process of searching for better images, adding crisper images, deleting unnecessary images, and connecting the images engages everyone. In other words, it's a shared picture that *everyone* has helped to create. It becomes a tremendous catalyst that sparks rapid innovation, widespread alignment, and unified ownership.

We've watched this occur hundreds of times in environments that are very political and formal. But with visual iteration, people begin to forget their biases and become childlike in their search and "idea hitchhiking." Invariably, the final visual is infinitely better than what any individual could come up with.

4. VISUAL ITERATION REDUCES DETAIL AND ADDS DEPTH. As it simplifies, visual iteration emphasizes the real meaning. When great sculptors are asked to explain how they create their masterpieces, most say that they simply "free the statue that's already in the marble." They see their task as just chipping away impurities. Essentially, sculpting is eliminating irrelevant material, getting rid of distractions, removing the superfluous—and by reducing detail, allowing the greatness to emerge.

Visual iteration works in this way too. The process begins with everyone piling their own details onto a page in an attempt to include all the best thoughts and ideas. The evolution starts when more details are added, to a point at which the "Where's Waldo?" designer would be proud. The initial picture becomes a confusing conglomeration: disconnected, disjointed, and chaotic. But as the thinking gets crisper, the picture gets sharper. Sometimes people need to see complexity before they can discover simplicity. As the picture evolves, less becomes more. And all this happens because people have found a way to think together by looking at the quality of their thoughts and building on them to make them better.

5. VISUAL ITERATION GIVES PEOPLE A COMMON LANGUAGE FOR CONVERSATION THAT ALLOWS THEM TO TALK TO EACH OTHER IN A WAY THAT'S UNPRECEDENTED. We've established that the written and spoken word is open to considerable misinterpretation. When people try to create or comprehend strategy or even figure out how their job or role fits into an organization, there is ample room for misunderstanding and confusion. The imprecise nature of verbal language perpetuates this, but the language of iterative visuals can surpass the weakness of words.

Not only does the quality of the ideas change, but so does the quality of the way in which groups interact to create them. When they've experienced this technique, people say, "We've never talked like this before. We've never shared ideas. We've never brought out the best in each other like this." And then: "Instead of using this approach to just sketch strategy, why don't we incorporate this as our day-to-day language to make better decisions?"

Visual iteration helps you "know it when you see it." And when you see it together, you're bound to make it much better.

QUESTIONS FOR ACTION

1. *Think of your best napkin sketch experience, whether you were the artist or were asked to review someone else's drawings. What drew you into the conversation? How did the napkin sketch help?*

2. *In the fable about the blind men and the elephant, the pieces that each one touched were determined to be the whole thing. Are you currently facing a problem like this? What picture could be drawn to reveal the entire "elephant"?*

3. *In engaging others in the stories of the business, how much time do you spend just trying to be sure you're all talking about the same thing? How much time do you spend trying to understand other perspectives? Could visual iteration redirect some of this time to the search for a better solution?*

4. *Visual iteration, like a good napkin sketch, has the potential to launch a new strategy, a new product, a new way to go to market, or a new plan to organize for success. How could you use napkin sketching to evoke simplicity, ownership, and thinking big?*

5. *What is one challenge in your business that people may not be seeing in the same way or thinking about with the same meaning? Could you leverage the restaurant example by taking pictures, posting them on the wall and, as a team, choosing the image that best represents the outcome you're trying to create?*

6. *Now, experiment by actually drawing a napkin sketch of your marketplace. Think about your business and the forces in the external marketplace. Determine the top five marketplace forces or stories that will most affect your business in the future. Grab a paper napkin (or use the one we've provided) and, using arrows, stick figures, and shapes, sketch the drama or big picture of your marketplace. You can make this sketch very simple; just be sure that it draws attention to the areas you want to emphasize. Then, find a colleague or two and explain the sketch to them. Ask them if they have any questions. Based on those questions and comments, edit or redraw*

Here's your napkin—start sketching!

your napkin sketch together. After you're done, consider what you learned. How can you use this simple sketch to help people understand the reasons why you need to change and the importance of successfully implementing your strategy?

chapter

12

Key #3: Believing in Leaders

Few people are more famous for sketching reality than Scott Adams, creator of the cartoon character Dilbert. Adams shows us the misadventures of the hapless victims of reengineering, right-sizing, and Total Quality Management and suggests some ideas for fighting back or, at the very least, coping. Clearly, Adams has struck a chord. Since its debut in 1989, *Dilbert* has been published in 1,900 newspapers in 57 countries, and translated into 19 languages. That's universal appeal!

In illustrating the trials of Dilbert, Adams vividly shows the pointless bureaucracies, rules, control mechanisms, and management fads that get in the way of real people doing real work. *Dilbert* gives people a voice, and they rally around that voice to address issues that frustrate them. His daily depictions of cubicle life ring true with so many people that it's hard to find an office without at least one *Dilbert* clipping tacked to the wall. They attract attention because of their truthfulness.

If there is a flaw in people's identification with the *Dilbert* world, it's that the cartoons perpetuate cynicism and stop short of finding a better way.

THE TRUTH REQUIRES TRUST

It's hard to authentically engage people if we aren't telling each other the truth. In *The Speed of Trust*, Stephen M. R. Covey says that trust is the most powerful form of motivation and inspiration in organizations, and that it's the ultimate source of influence. On the reverse side, however, low trust slows decision-making, communications, relationships, and results. Mistrust is more the norm than the exception. Covey presents the following statistics:

- Only 51% of employees trust their senior management.
- Only 36% of employees believe that their leaders act with honesty.
- Only 27% of people today trust the government.
- And just 12% of people trust big companies.

Covey's conclusion is that no quality is more important or more rare than trust.

The successful engagement of people requires authenticity, truth telling, and realism. It all starts by defining reality and having the courage to accept it at face value. There are three beliefs that explain why this happens:

- People think that their managers and leaders really don't want to hear the truth.
- People don't believe that they can safely tell the truth.
- People don't know how to discuss the "undiscussable" issues and still be viewed as a positive force in the organization.

All of these beliefs continue to be responsible for the lack of realism and truth in our day-to-day interactions. They force people to say what they think others want to hear, rather than what they really believe to be true. As a result, we don't become real in our expectations, in our thinking, and in our interactions. Much of this typical "engagement" ends up being nothing more than a charade.

VISUALIZING TRUTH TO FIND A BETTER WAY

To engage people in strategies and create better business results, organizations require discussions that are authentic and real. Most companies and teams don't know how to have these conversations.

One of the most longed-for aspects of truth telling is just the simple acknowledgment of "how we're doing." A senior executive of a company that had elevated good manners to master black belt status told me this: "We just need to acknowledge where we are off the mark. Our people talk past each other, point fingers, and generally avoid the brutal facts that we need to embrace. We've lost the art of being straightforward, simple, and engaged."

It's in discussions like these that teams begin to take their performance to the next level. Critical conversations *should* happen in the open. But in many organizations, they occur in just three places—at the water cooler, in the restrooms, and in the hallways. Those are the locations where people feel free to say what they really think, and where they can share their views and speak the truth.

As we've worked with various companies, we've created some techniques to move these hidden conversations into public dialogue.

Places where we feel safe speaking the truth.

One technique is called "water cooler sketching." After leaders tell us about the obstacles and challenges they face, an artist draws a black-and-white characterization of these problems or barriers. Using compelling visual caricatures, cartoonlike quote bubbles, and humor, these sketches get to the heart of the matter in a way that mere words can't. The light tone ensures that no one takes the organizational self-critique too seriously.

These water cooler sketches create a candid mirror of reality. They are an informal way to address conflict, ambiguities in the strategy, and destructive behaviors, and offer opportunities for

> **Water cooler sketches create a candid mirror of reality.**

individuals and teams to be more effective. They invite people to openly talk about the tough issues. The sketches "draw out" opinions, attitudes, and beliefs so that they can be honestly addressed and so that new solutions can be crafted. People simply can't look at the picture and decide not to do anything about it.

Let's look at some real examples of how water cooler sketches have helped companies deal with tough engagement challenges.

SEPARATING ISSUES FROM INDIVIDUALS

We recently worked with a large utility company whose leaders were extraordinarily polite and diplomatic in the way they dealt with each other. (The joke was that each manager had a box of "politeness tissues" to use when working with colleagues in-house.) The leaders often acted ugly behind the scenes and were courteous only in public. This only-in-public polite behavior had become a convenient crutch for avoiding disagreement and conflict. However, when they needed to discuss a difficult topic, they had no idea how to have the conversation.

This conflict-avoidance behavior hampered the leaders' ability to execute even the most mundane business changes. In extensive interviews, we found that their biggest problem was the inability to separate business issues from individuals. This was prevalent in all areas of management, preventing people from making timely decisions and addressing competitive threats. Even more dangerous, the leaders had created a political atmosphere that kept people from ever knowing what colleagues were thinking. Truth telling was anything but a core competency.

To attempt to separate the issues from the individuals, our artists drew sketches. The first represented two significant business issues in a boxing ring. They are supposed to be debating the issues in order to arrive at the best decision. However, in the sketch, the issues aren't battling at all. They're practically asleep. And while nothing is happening in the ring, all of the people involved with these issues are fighting with each other in the stands! The hostile skirmishes of conflicting opinions look very personal and emotional.

Sketch 1: It can be hard to separate issues from individuals.

The visualization of this problem was a vehicle that opened genuine dialogue for the first time. It allowed the leaders and managers to talk about the dysfunctional behavior that was holding back the organization. People had confused talking about an *issue* with talking about a *person*. If someone disagreed with a perspective, it was perceived as an assault on the one who suggested it. The team began to split into good guys and bad guys. Whenever people with differing perspectives tried to talk about their ideas publicly, the discussion immediately got very loud and very personal and was promptly discontinued.

As this leadership team looked at the sketch, they began to realize that they *could* disagree on an issue and not be disagreeable to the person who proposed it. This distinction was a critical ingredient for having a rigorous debate before making decisions

Sketch 2: Visualizing reality lets the issues "battle to clarity."

on key business issues. Before long, the team was so committed to changing this reality that they asked us to draw a second sketch, to show what this *should* look like.

The second water cooler sketch shows the two issues in a very different light. This time, the issues are forcefully battling each other in order to achieve a decisive outcome. The people in the stands are aligning with one side or another and encouraging the active discussion of the issues. They are no longer involved in hand-to-hand combat because of their differences of opinion. The act of visualizing reality allowed people to see the need for a process to separate issues from individuals. This company still uses the language inspired by the sketches to refer to issues that need to be thoroughly debated and then "put into the ring" to "battle to clarity."

THE CHASM BETWEEN THE OLD GUARD AND THE NEW GUARD

Let's see how water cooler sketching can address a different kind of problem. A team at a financial services company was facing significant change. Because this team included veteran employees and new hires, the groups had begun to divide into an "old guard" and a "new guard." After talking to everyone on each side, our artists sketched their reality as a group of children playing in an "executive sandbox" (shown on the next page).

The motto of the old guard was, "We built this place and it's not all broken," and the new guard's mantra was, "We're the new talent for a new destination." Both guards were competing to make a big impact in the business instead of focusing on taking their company's performance to the next level. Both were striving to get the most sand to build their own castles instead of figuring out how to build one really great castle for the entire organization. Everyone suffered from a lack of direction, and others who were impacted by this dysfunctional team felt buried in ambiguity.

Hoarding "sand" instead of building one great castle.

When the groups saw the sketch, they recognized themselves. As the CEO said, "Something happens when people tell each other the truth. When we visualize reality, we become much more accountable and supportive of each other in our behaviors and actions to lead the business." The group learned that the seasoned executives as well as the new ones wanted to make a big impact individually, and their separate agendas kept them from blending the best that both groups had to offer for the future. The old guard understood the industry, the financial service business, and the inherent risks. The new guard brought nonfinancial business innovation, enhanced process excellence, and a refreshing urgency to act. In the end, the team needed all these attributes to win.

CHANGING THE IMAGE OF REALITY

In companies around the world, water cooler sketches of reality are teaching people how to engage in the critical conversations that they previously didn't know how to have. They allow people at all levels to step into the conflict that's holding them back from achieving better business results.

It's important to remember that sketching the truth is valuable *only* if it deepens accountability, challenges the status quo, and enables new energy and enthusiasm for finding a better way. In each of the cases we've discussed, and in dozens of others, water cooler sketches give people on any team the opportunity to put the truth on the table in a safe way. The process usually includes having the team add their own images and quotes to the existing sketch.

> **W**hen we visualize reality, we become much more accountable and supportive of each other.

In each case, team members are asked to select the most real components of the sketch that need to be addressed. More than that, they are asked to identify how they've contributed to the truth on the table, what they need to do to change that behavior, and how the future sketch of the company's reality should look.

In the *Dilbert* cartoons, the cynicism and frustration imply that someone else needs to do something about the current reality. But the water cooler sketch process forces people to realize that they are *all* accountable for creating and sustaining the environment that needs to change. The key is to use the sketch to start a conversation that, in the end, is about how reality must change—and that change starts with the leaders of the organization.

QUESTIONS FOR ACTION

Think about the challenges and realities facing your organization. Does your company look like the water cooler sketching examples from this chapter? If not, draw your own sketch (even if it's only on a napkin) and invite people to look at it and to discuss the undiscussables. One simple way to do this is to draw "the elephant in the room." (Or you can use the one we've provided here.) Ask people to determine the issues that have not been addressed and are holding the group back from greater performance, and write them directly on the elephant. Another equally valuable way to "discuss the undiscussables" is to personalize the generic water cooler sketch found at www.rootsofengagement.com. This sketch can accommodate unique quotes and comments that can help you set the stage for a productive conversation.

Here are some of the questions you might ask when your team is looking at your napkin sketch, the words on the elephant, or your water cooler sketch:

1.   What gets discussed at our water cooler?
2.   What images or quotes would you add?
3.   Does this sketch of reality impact our business? If so, how?

What elephants are in your room?

4. Which images or quotes are most relevant to you?
5. How have we contributed to this picture?
6. How have we benefited from this picture?
7. Why are we perpetuating this picture?
8. How likely are we to succeed if we don't change this picture?
9. Considering all the realities in the sketch, what would you title the picture?
10. How should the picture change to make sure we're successful in engaging people on the truth of our current reality?

chapter

13

Key #4: Owning
the Solution

From young to old, most people have an insatiable appetite for solving things that need solving. Toddlers try to fit square pegs into square holes and round pegs into round ones. As we grow, we move on to assemble jigsaw puzzles, from 24 pieces to 1,000. Teenagers may not realize it, but video games are basically interactive puzzle boards that ask the player to navigate courses, make decisions, and ultimately determine the right choices so they can amass the highest score. Crossword puzzle fanatics are everywhere, and it's not uncommon to see an adult scribbling in a Sudoku book. Novels such as those by James Patterson are puzzles, too, ones that keep readers guessing how the characters and plots fit together and will evolve.

All of these puzzles invite people to think independently, to challenge their assumptions, and to make guesstimates about what's next. What's common to all these examples is that people are engaged in forging new connections and relationships to successfully solve the puzzle. Whether it's competitive or not, puzzle solving is a highly focused and compelling way to expand people's ability to think, reason, and connect information. When the 2-year-old stands up and yells as all the blocks fall into the right positions, when the 15-year-old masters the latest video game, or when the professor solves the *New York Times* Sunday crossword in record time, each one feels a sense of satisfaction that comes from making critical connections. The pride of solving the problem "by yourself" is unmistakable.

This is what some educators call *discovery learning*, or actively participating in the learning process rather than passively receiving knowledge. The passive learning role, common in many organizations, has been described as the "mug-and-jug" theory: If you sit still long enough, the person with the knowledge in his jug will pour it into your mug. But discovery learning provides the knowledge and tools that people need to "mine" information so that they can understand a concept or solve a problem. It stops short of presenting a conclusion. Discovery learning requires people to ask questions, develop their own tentative answers, and glean concepts from practical examples. As a result, people convert these concepts into new understandings that make sense—specifically, that make sense to *them*. Scientists tell us that the brain

Dumping information can't spark "discovery learning."

is constantly searching for meaningful relationships to connect disconnected pieces into a whole. That's the "aha."

AHA! MOMENTS

In each step of searching for answers, insights created from discovering a connection lead us toward solving the puzzle. These insights cause people to think differently about the entire puzzle. This begins with trial and error, by asking, "What's the best way to do this?" It's experimenting with one choice that doesn't totally work and asking the question again to see if there's a different way to look at it, and continuing to evolve the thinking about how all the pieces fit together. Each question leads to a new probe, a new search, and the possibility of a new connection. This is how puzzles work, and it's why they're so captivating and engaging.

Now, anyone could just look up the answers to a puzzle before they start. So why doesn't this happen very often? The truth is, people *want* to figure it out for themselves. If it were just about finding the right answer, we'd simply read the final chapter of the mystery novel or scan the blog that shows how to master the video game.

But it's more than that. Without search and discovery, there is no feeling of accomplishment. There is no journey, so our thinking doesn't expand throughout the process. In the end, there is no adventure and no new learning. And true engagement really *does* require adventure. People want to develop the confidence and capability to handle their own problems. This confidence then encourages them to attempt even tougher puzzles. Real engagement is born when the responsibility for solving business challenges or puzzles shifts from the makers of the strategy to the implementers of strategy.

> **True engagement really *does* require adventure.**

So when it comes to business puzzles, why do leaders often assume that the best way to engage people is to merely show them the answer book? When those "answers" are presented in passive vehicles such as PowerPoint presentations, comprehensive speeches, or detailed letters, leaders skip the major step that allows people to make the critical connections to solve the puzzle. People don't want to be told what to think or just be shown the answer key. They want to be actively involved in the process of searching and exploring, considering and dismissing, and challenging and repositioning beliefs about how the business works.

> **People don't want to be told what to think or just be shown the answer key.**

As we've said, people will tolerate the conclusions of their leaders, but they will act on their own. So, if people are going to change their conclusions, leaders must let them take an active role in solving the business puzzles. People simply won't let others change their conclusions *for* them.

SOCRATES, THE MASTER PUZZLER

Centuries ago, Socrates knew that learning was a matter of asking the right questions to get to core truths. Instead of presenting conclusions, he immersed people in exploration and inquiry that allowed them to answer their own questions. Socrates called this "dialogue." In *The Fifth Discipline*, Peter Senge called out the difference between various types of conversations. The word *discussion* has the same root as does *percussion* and suggests a rather forceful "throwing" of ideas at others. But dialogue, Senge points out, comes from two Greek words—*dia*, or "across," and *logus*, or "word." Thus, "the meaning comes across."

Socrates often engaged small groups of people so that the dialogue didn't occur within just one person's head (as some puzzles require). In these small groups, each member added a new perspective. By its very nature, dialogue demands that people challenge their cherished assumptions and objectively examine their long-held beliefs. This is exactly how we can engage people in business to create better results.

All businesses are constantly working to solve their ever-changing business puzzles. These require as much thought, trial and error, reflection, and, in the end, connections as the most mind-stretching competitive puzzles in other areas of life. The key tool for solving these is the use of strategic, Socratic dialogue. This doesn't mean a wide-open, free-for-all session with random questions on a wide range of issues. It *does* mean that the questions are directed and connected to the strategy.

The questions are *strategic* because they're often selected or prioritized by leaders or teams who have spent time researching and analyzing the business. They are the same tough questions that the leaders have tried to address. The object is to have everyone in the company go down the same road of critical thinking on the business imperatives. And the questions must remain *Socratic*, which suggests that there are no exact right-or-wrong answers. There is, however, constant alignment and refinement of the *best* answers for the current environment.

WHAT ARE THE RIGHT QUESTIONS?

Before choosing questions to ask, think about this bold statement: "The world we think we live in no longer exists." Why? Because by the time we realize what's going on, things have changed! Most people walk around with pictures in their heads that help make sense of the world and their role in it. In simple terms, these pictures represent current beliefs and conclusions. But there's a tremendous time lapse between what's developed in people's heads and reality. That's why engagement and discovery learning are so critical for synching up the pictures in people's heads with the actual pictures of the realities of the business.

The above figure, "5 Steps of Discovery," lays out a logical progression of how small groups of people can engage in strategic dialogue—dialogue that will create discoveries that truly change their conclusions about the way they see the business. Each step is a key element in allowing people to figure out for themselves how the business is changing and what needs to be done differently to be successful.

Tapping into people's curiosity, aligning with the latest "stories" told by the data, seeing the business as a holistic system, developing new mental pictures or conclusions, and then applying those new conclusions to real-life challenges is exactly what people must do if they are going to execute a strategy. This process is all about dialogue, discovery, engagement, and building everyone's ability to personalize the business strategy. When all this happens, people are doing exactly what they do when they solve any other puzzle; they're putting themselves in a position to figure it out for themselves, creating ownership or buy-in, and generating excitement about practicing it in the real world.

Let's explore these five steps in a little more detail.

CURIOSITY. These questions draw out what people really want to know. Curiosity taps into what's relevant to people's perceptions or assumptions about the business, so these are the questions that spark that curiosity. They awaken interest and are relevant to people at every level of the business. They are questions like these:

- How much money does the business make out of a dollar of revenue?
- Who are our biggest customers?
- How much money is tied up in inventory?
- Who are the newest customer segments?
- How much money do we waste in the manufacturing process?

DATA STORIES. After interest and relevance are established, the next step is to provide information, or "data stories." Data stories show the trends and direction that a key issue is taking. The questions are attached to data that helps people understand the ebbs and flows of the business. They represent the hard facts that people can contemplate to start the process of reconsidering or unlearning old perceptions of the business and opening their minds to new ideas. These hard facts are best represented as trend lines that are going up, going down, or staying flat. Each of these trend lines brings a different sense of urgency to the business. Some examples:

- How will the aging population trend impact our business in the future?
- What are the underlying reasons behind the margin decline in three of our five primary markets?

- When you consider the trend toward continually shrinking product life cycle, how will the timeframe affect our product launches in the future?

SYSTEMS ANALYSIS. Because most of business is about systems, and people rarely think in terms of systems, questions that consider the data stories and business systems are extremely important. They prompt people to compare old and new information, relationships, and pictures. The combination of data stories and systems analysis is crucial to processing existing knowledge with new information. In this way, we can examine and consider different conclusions from those we started with. In crossword puzzle terms, this is the stage where, when you solve 2 Across, 3 Down begins to make a lot of sense. It includes unlearning, making new connections, openly challenging assumptions, and laying the groundwork for entirely new conclusions. Many of these questions begin with "What do you think . . . ?" They call into play people's assumptions and experiences and expand them into a bigger *systems* context. Some examples:

- What do you think the competition would do if we raised our prices? (Be mindful that the answers must consider market share issues, margin issues, and future growth issues, all of which are part of a system.)
- Which of our annual growth figures surprises you the most, and why?
- What do you think is behind the recent surge in volume?
- Which of these factors do you think will have the biggest impact on our organization?

NEW PICTURES. By combining curiosity, data stories, and systems analysis, new conclusions spring to life. These new mental pictures are what cause people to change their opinions, alter their beliefs, and be open to behaving differently. When conclusions change, behavioral changes often follow. Questions that help develop new pictures are those that encourage people to draw inferences from their new information, dialogue, and connections. This is where people replace what they believed to be true *before* with what they *now* see. These questions require people to use what was learned from the first three steps to draw new conclusions. Instead of asking, "What do you think?" these questions often ask, "How do you see it all fitting together?" Examples of this kind of question include:

- When you consider our historical pricing trends, the new pricing pressures in our marketplace, and customers' recent reactions to our latest pricing changes, do you believe that we'll be able to raise our prices in the near future?
- Think about changing consumer expectations, the rapid increase in our product offerings, and the new standards on the speed of delivery. How must our customer fulfillment process change in the future?
- Consider the decline in some of our most profitable customer segments and the growth in volume of some of our least profitable customer groups. What should we focus on for the future—profit or volume?

PRACTICE. In this step, people are asked to apply their new conclusions to the challenges and opportunities in front of them. Practice requires the effort of applying those new pictures and conclusions to the challenges of the business by asking, "How can we change?" These kinds of questions encourage people to identify new actions that can create even better results. By answering these questions, people rehearse the actions and consequences that might be attempted as a result of the insights generated from the Steps of Discovery. Some examples:

- How could we better differentiate ourselves in the market-place?
- How could we reduce the amount of inventory in our work-in-process?
- How could we accelerate new product development and launches?
- How could we better execute on our solutions strategy?

This five-step process allows everyone to go on an exciting journey where they consider and challenge, dialogue and discuss, learn and unlearn, and ultimately come to new insights on how the business works. These new insights open their minds to the changes that must be undertaken for the business to succeed. More than just understanding these changes, the five-step process allows people to be immersed in them. The involvement in each step goes far beyond building understanding; it elicits ownership and commitment.

THE DISCOVERY STEPS IN ACTION

Here's a real example of how a group of employees went through each step of the discovery process and, in so doing, changed their approach to engaging in and executing their strategy.

The leaders of an East Coast glass products manufacturing company were attempting to get their people to be more effective regarding plant operations. At a town hall meeting, one of the managers asked the employees, "Based on what you see in the business, what are you curious about?" Several members of the workforce were confused by reports of financial results that didn't seem to match the level of activity and volume in the factory. One employee said, "How come we're working so hard and making so little profit?" Another employee followed up with this: "Where are all of our products going, and what difference does the destination make in how much we get paid for them?" This set off other questions such as, "Why do we implement rapid line changeovers for certain customers and not for other ones?" and "Should we favor certain customers over others?" Behind each of these questions was employee *curiosity* about what was going on in the business. This prompted the manager to ask the group what they thought the profit actually was for each type of customer, what they thought the sales volume was for each type of customer, and which types of customers valued speed of response more than the others. Because the answers from the employees (which represented their "pictures" of how the business worked) were so disconnected from reality, the next town hall meeting focused on three *data stories*—the profit generated by each customer segment, the volume for each customer segment, and the value that each customer segment placed on customization and speed of delivery.

Once employees had the opportunity to discuss this information with their leaders and see all of it together as a package (*systems analysis*), they came to a whole new level of understanding. People learned that the business had three very different customer segments: a discount retail segment that had 60 percent of the volume but generated less than 20 percent of the profit; a restaurant segment with 20 percent of the volume and 30 percent of the profit; and a highly customized hotel segment that represented 20 percent of the volume but more than 50 percent of the profit. In the process, employees had the opportunity to further pursue these questions in dialogue sessions with a cross-section of peers. Employees talked about the importance of volume and profit, the expectations of standard and custom products for each customer group, and the overall performance of the business (*new pictures*).

Then, employees began to *practice*, and something happened that leaders hadn't expected. Their new clarity about the business inspired engagement, which led to a sense of empowerment. The employees asked what they could do to maximize the line turnovers for the "custom" customers who were willing to pay the highest premium for their products, and also how they could help minimize the costs in running the volume for customers who paid the least for their products. All of this went far beyond previous attempts by managers to improve changeover times and reduce waste. After this experience, one senior leader commented that the combination of discovery and dialogue is the true "oxygen of engagement." He said that this combination is what makes great conversations.

BETTER RESULTS

Why does engaging people in dialogue and discovery create better business results? It's because people use their personal associations to learn rather than having to accept someone else's thoughts at face value. People pay more attention because they actively participate rather than just halfheartedly listen and follow directions. When curiosity, current data stories, systems analysis, and group dialogue are combined, people readily change the way they picture their business. They change their own conclusions and are motivated to act on these new conclusions. The new pictures are far more likely to be retained because they're self-developed and built in a real-life context.

QUESTIONS FOR ACTION

1. *What puzzles of your business do you think your people are most interested in solving for themselves? Have you asked them?*

2. *In which areas of the business have you tried to show people the "answer key" and then been frustrated when they didn't show any interest?*

3. *Where are you still telling and selling and thus preventing people from engaging in actively solving business puzzles?*

4. *What are the current business puzzles that you're trying to solve? How could you effectively present your people with the*

same questions you've wrestled with so that they can make the answers their own and take the necessary actions also on their own (or even find answers that are better than yours)?

5. *How could you use the Steps of Discovery (curiosity, data stories, systems analysis, new pictures, and practice) to engage your people to better execute your business strategy?*

chapter

14

Key #5: Playing the Entire Game

In sports or in business, people really want to be "in the game"—they don't want to just sit on the sidelines as spectators. They want to be part of the adventure of their business. In 1985, John Fogerty, of Creedence Clearwater Revival fame, recorded a memorable song about baseball called "Centerfield." While it never became the official theme song for the Cleveland Indians, you'd have a hard time attending an Indians game where they didn't play it at least once. The key lines go, "Put me in, coach, I'm ready to play . . . I spent some time watching from the bench . . . don't say it ain't so, you know the time is now . . . Put me in coach, I'm ready to play."

People in business want the same thing—the chance to play in a real game where everyone can show what they can do to contribute to a victory. But how can business leaders create a playing field that allows everyone in the company to share their point of view, have that viewpoint valued, and not be threatened or judged for their opinions? How do you go beyond simply giving out information and inspire people to act?

Businesses work best when the parameters are clear to everyone, the scoring is understood, the outcomes that define winning are outlined, the tools of information gathering are available, and everyone is invited to play. One of the best ways to accomplish this is with a tool called a *Learning Map*® visual. These "pictures" have a brilliant way of allowing people to see the big picture and tiny details at the same time. By using this tool, business leaders *can* engage people in something bigger than themselves—leaders *can* get their people in the game.

MAPPING TO THE WAY PEOPLE LEARN

Before people can play, they need to learn about the game. And even though we all have similar brains, we all learn in different ways. The right and left hemispheres of the brain interpret information differently. Some people are more logical or analytical, and prefer to dissect the world into parts. These are "left-brained" people. Others are more intuitive or subjective, and begin the thinking process by looking at the whole. These are the "right-brained" people. Some are equally adept at both modes, but most have a preference for one side or the other. Additionally, certain types of learners prefer to receive information in one of three ways—visually, auditorily, or kinesthetically. Again, people tend to use all of these styles, but most have a bias for a primary style.

When we consider the different learning styles, we can see why engagement can be sporadic with many employees. So to engage a wide range of people in any organization, the learning experience must appeal to all learning styles and both hemispheres of the brain, casting a wide net to catch everyone's personal preference. It has to work for everybody, because business success depends on all employees. By relating to how people learn, it's possible to create a way to effectively engage every person in an organization. When done properly, each person should believe that the *Learning Map*® was created especially for them.

> **The learning experience must cast a wide net.**

THE *LEARNING MAP*® EXPERIENCE

The *Learning Map*® visual that we first referred to in Chapter 10 is actually the focal point of a total learning experience. The *Learning*

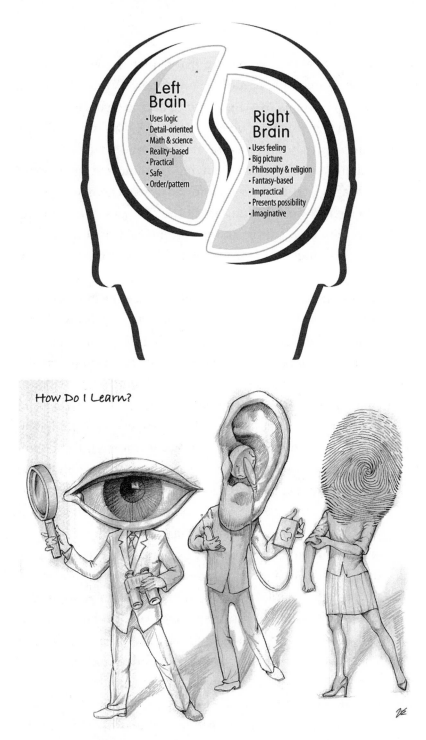

How Do I Learn?

Leaders need to appeal to all kinds of learners.

Map® visual is a table-sized picture that depicts an entire business or business system in a graphic metaphor. While the visual metaphor can be subjective (right brain), data in charts and graphs embedded in the visual are objective facts (left brain). In all, the picture speaks to both types of thinkers and invites both to explore their business. Accompanying Socratic questions drive dialogue that is vital to the search for answers. The questions are written to elicit critical thinking about the company and its future, not to proclaim dogma from top management. It is this dialogue that is the real engine of engagement. The *Learning Map*® visual allows people to understand their business stories, arrive at their own conclusions, and expand their ability to see the big picture of the business. The visuals, often referred to as "maps," draw together all of the elements we've been discussing. They provide a simple, actionable path for engaging people in tackling virtually any issue that a company needs to address. Here's how it works.

A small group of people—typically 8 to 10—gather around the map and discuss what they see (for visual learners), guided by strategically directed dialogue (for auditory learners). Just seeing the entire business illustrated in a map elicits a huge aha from most people because it takes something that's often been discussed in words, but never with the detail and completeness that a picture provides, and makes it visual and tangible.

Working as a group, participants use cards to rank, match, or order data and information (for kinesthetic learners). The information on the cards and on charts printed on the map itself represents the most critical and strategic issues in the business that people really need to understand and take action on. It's the one place where, as with any map, people can understand the whole, see the entire panorama, and truly grasp the complexities of the business challenges they face.

The entire experience is designed to enable people to come to their own conclusions. Because these are *their own conclusions*, people move to action much more readily. They do this by answering questions such as "Considering what you've just learned, what is one thing that you can start (or stop) doing that will make an impact on the business?" The focus is on the local level, on things that people can actually implement without first getting permission from top leadership to do. The goal is for individuals to imple-

> **Seeing the entire business illustrated in a map elicits a huge "aha" from most people.**

ment as many of their own ideas as possible—that's what makes the experience so empowering.

Like any map for a journey whose route isn't initially clear, *Learning Map®* visuals provide a focus that helps people to plot their journey and fully realize the steps they need to take to arrive at a desired destination. When people understand that they have the ability to be in the game on their own, they will be inspired again and again.

While water cooler sketches capture the emotion and drama of the canyons between people and their leaders or managers and give everyone a way to talk about the undiscussables, *Learning Map®* visuals create the practice field for the mental workouts that will get leaders, managers, and individuals ready to truly bridge those canyons.

COMPONENTS OF THE *LEARNING MAP®* MODULE

A *Learning Map®* module has just four elements: visualization, data and information cards, peer dialogue in small groups, and facilitation. To get a sense of what it looks like when people engage in a *Learning Map®* experience, look at the photos on the next two pages.

Visualization—the picture itself—is the first thing that catches the eye, and it resembles a traditional map. Icons, infographics, and metaphors combine to frame a business system. Because the

Data Connections

Facilitation

The Group

Dialogue Questions

The Visual

Card Exercises

The components of a Learning Map® *experience.*

visual *does* frame a systems perspective, it forces everyone to think holistically. Therefore, the visuals become "brain gyms" that allow groups to compare and contrast, challenge and reconsider, and learn together what is critical to the business.

The second element is *data or information cards*. These allow people to explore information in layers so they can more easily break down complex issues into simple pieces that make sense. In this way, understanding builds slowly for people, rather than the hit-or-miss prospect of having to get it all at once. This also allows them to see how any change in one layer of data can impact the overall business system.

But a systems visual and data or information cards alone can't draw out new conclusions. This occurs only during the process of *peer dialogue* and discovery, the third component of the *Learning Map®* module. Peer dialogue involves learning about business systems and the business itself in a small group by pursuing strategic questions about the business and its operations. Because the questions are Socratic, the group learns together until they can see the

A Learning Map® session in action.

business as a system, share their own knowledge and experiences, and affirm or support the new insights that result from the conversation. Together, the group uses their new insights to identify practical actions to improve the business.

The last component of the module is *facilitation*. The facilitator encourages the group to uncover the ahas of the business and translate the strategy into something that's relevant to them. Facilitators guide the conversation without introducing their own thoughts or opinions. They encourage independent search and discovery rather than imparting knowledge. If the facilitator becomes "the teacher," the search shuts down, limiting what can be truly learned.

Now, let's look at four real-life *Learning Map®* modules and some of the questions and cards that guided learners through them.

PEPSI-COLA'S STRATEGIC SHIFT

Some time ago, Pepsi-Cola made a strategic shift to become a "total beverage company." At the time, this was a significant change from its long tradition of focusing on carbonated soft drinks. The shift would affect the roles and responsibilities of everyone within the business.

After several attempts to communicate the new strategy in traditional ways, Pepsi leaders were still getting significant resistance from all levels of the workforce. Common responses to the push for change included, "We don't need new products—we just need to advertise more" and "We only have four bays on our trucks and they're already full with Pepsi, Diet Pepsi, Mountain Dew, and Diet Mountain Dew." New products such as Snapple were seen as faddish; their packaging was bulky and breakable, and the employees didn't see how they would generate the volume needed for financial incentives. The execution of the new strategy to become a total beverage company was stuck. In an attempt to build employees' understanding of the changing dynamics of the business and the need to shift to become a total beverage company, Pepsi worked with us to create a set of three *Learning Map*® modules.

The modules were intended to create a mind-set shift for all Pepsi employees from apathy, indifference, and resistance to an informed sense of urgency. The first module, called "Revolution on Beverage Street," had to effectively engage people in the elements of the drama that was playing out "on the streets" of the business. These included:

1. The decline in carbonated soft drink growth.
2. The explosion of variety in packaging and beverages.
3. The aging population and their declining carbonated soft drink consumption patterns.
4. Increasing demands for health, convenience, variety, and value.
5. Expansion and improvement of the quality of private label competition.
6. The decline of carbonated soft drink pricing and a widening gap between this pricing and overall inflation.

The *"big picture"* of Pepsi-Cola's marketplace.

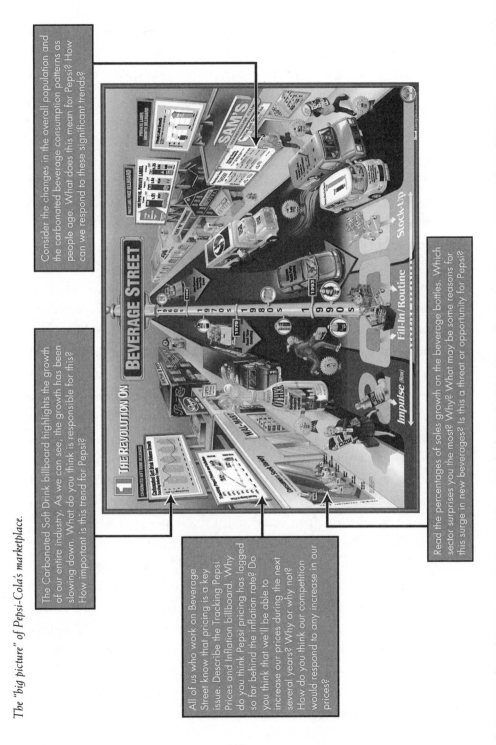

The Carbonated Soft Drink billboard highlights the growth of our entire industry. As we can see, the growth has been slowing down. What do you think is responsible for this? How important is this trend for Pepsi?

Consider the changes in the overall population and the carbonated beverage consumption patterns as people age. What does this mean for Pepsi? How can we respond to these significant trends?

All of us who work on Beverage Street know that pricing is a key issue. Describe the Tracking Pepsi Prices and Inflation billboard. Why do you think Pepsi pricing has lagged so far behind the inflation rate? Do you think that we'll be able to increase our prices during the next several years? Why or why not? How do you think our competition would respond to any increase in our prices?

Read the percentages of sales growth on the beverage bottles. Which sector surprises you the most? Why? What may be some reasons for this surge in new beverages? Is this a threat or opportunity for Pepsi?

143

7. The emergence of three purchase occasions that had unique value propositions.

8. The combination of these forces to create robust threats and opportunities for everyone in the industry.

In summary, consumer behavior was changing, and the company knew they needed to change in response.

The *Learning Map*® visual (shown in color at the center of the book) graphically captured all of these changing dynamics. The story of how Pepsi got 34,000 frontline employees engaged in the strategy of their business is best told by Sue Tsokris, vice president, general manager at Pepsi, who at the time was intimately involved in engaging Pepsi's people in this critical change. "Employees were resisting the change and asking, 'Do we really have to do all these things differently?'" she said. "The beauty of the maps was that they created a level playing field that enabled everyone in the company to talk about the business, regardless of rank or function. All points of view mattered equally—everyone felt valued and no one felt threatened or judged when they expressed their ideas.

"It was interesting to watch the discussion dynamics evolve during the *Learning Map*® exercises," said Tsokris, "from tense and wary to engaged and energized, from cautious and watchful to open and trusting. You could tell it made people feel important, and they realized that they could learn from each other. They quickly saw that everyone had a piece of the puzzle that we were trying to assemble. It also helped us challenge the prevailing belief that learning is boring and one-way, and requires you to just sit and listen. Instead, it offered the possibility that much of the know-how we needed was in the heads and experiences of our people.

"What was most exhilarating was that not only did coworkers engage completely and enjoy the learning experience, but they felt valued. They felt important. And you could tell they *got it*.

They started talking about what we needed to do differently as a business to better position ourselves for the future. They talked about the importance of moving quickly to make these changes. You could feel the energy around the table, and you knew that they wanted to be part of the change. You knew they felt compelled to do their part. It gave me goose bumps!"

Tsokris continued, "For us, change needs to be implemented 'inside-out'—as in a microwave rather than a traditional oven, sort of from the head and heart out. People have to think about the change, figure out how they feel about it, and want to do something different before change happens. The *Learning Map*® modules did this for us."

According to Tsokris, people emerged from the experience feeling more informed about the business and more interested in and capable of changing the way they approached the business from within their own roles. Company strategies were embraced as urgent and critical, and people felt more motivated to focus on and achieve the necessary results.

HARLEY-DAVIDSON'S BUSINESS ECONOMICS

All employees need an in-depth understanding of the economics of the company—where the money comes from, where it goes, and how much the company gets to keep. Most organizations benefit from employees who see how they can generate more revenue, reduce expenses, and enhance the bottom line. Harley-Davidson is one of these companies.

In his book, *More Than a Motorcycle*, Rich Teerlink, former chairman of Harley-Davidson, explains the role that *Learning Map*® modules played in the transformation of the entire business. To assist in this transformation, maps were created to address several topics, including the money cycle. The map on the next page (and at the center of the book) was designed to show how Harley-Davidson makes and spends money and the key measures that

Harley-Davidson's financial flow.

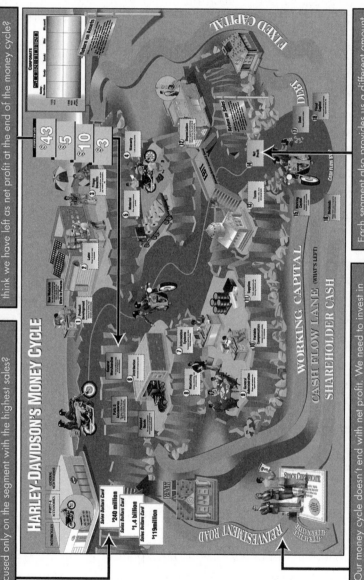

Our three product segments are Motorcycles, Parts and Accessories, and General Merchandise. Each segment provides a different amount of sales dollars. Let's match the **Sales Dollars cards** to the correct segments. What do you think would happen if Harley-Davidson focused only on the segment with the highest sales?

Let's find out how much we spend on our various expenses. As a group, we'll place an **Expense Run card** on correct areas. Where in the money cycle do we have the best opportunity to save one dollar? Based on $100, how much money do you think we have left as net profit at the end of the money cycle?

Each segment also provides us a different amount of profit, or the sales dollars minus our expenses. Which segment do you think brings in the most?

Our money cycle doesn't end with net profit. We need to invest in the future. What would be the result if we failed to reinvest? What eventually happens to the money we reinvest in the business?

HARLEY-DAVIDSON'S MONEY CYCLE

MOTORCYCLES

PARTS & ACCESSORIES

GENERAL MERCHANDISE

Sales Dollars Card
$240 million

Sales Dollars Card
$1.4 billion

Sales Dollars Card
$115 million

$43
$5
$10
$3

FIXED CAPITAL

DEBT

Return on Assets

Return on Sales

WORKING CAPITAL

CASH FLOW LANE (WHAT'S LEFT)

SHAREHOLDER CASH

REINVESTMENT ROAD

influence the money flow. This concept was important for everyone to understand so that they could appreciate the role they played in affecting the financial outcomes of the business.

At the time, Harley's business was experiencing many changes. The need for everyone to understand the overall business economics became more important to its success. Harley's revenue streams were coming from motorcycles, parts and accessories, and general merchandise. How the money from these revenue streams was used and the importance of continuing the predictability of these revenue streams was not widely known throughout the organization. Equally hidden were some key company elements such as the work-in-process and finished goods categories, where significant dollars were captured, and in return affected Harley's overall performance.

Teerlink, who was trained as a chief financial officer, wanted everyone to see the economics of the business much more clearly and see their own role in how well the Harley economic engine performed. In addition to the often invisible work-in-process and finished goods, Teerlink wanted everyone to understand the entire economic system, which included these components:

1. The sources of revenue: motorcycles, parts and accessories, and general merchandise.
2. All earnings before interest and tax expenses, such as product development, labor, material, marketing and distribution, etc.
3. The working capital needs of the business, often found in work-in-process and finished goods.
4. The debt repayment requirements that were key components of operating the business.
5. Fixed capital investments needed to continue to update and improve the assets of the business.
6. The cash flow required for the business to continue to meet its liquidity obligations.

7. The necessary amount of return for shareholders to maintain their investments in the company.

8. How Harley's performance in return on assets and return on sales compared with their chosen benchmark companies.

As a result, everyone at Harley-Davidson was able to have a common mind-set about the economics of the business. This mind-set went beyond knowing where the money came from and where it went. It illuminated the understanding that everyone's actions could be examined to better contribute to the overall economic performance of the business.

HAMPTON'S INITIATIVE LAUNCH

Not long ago, Hampton Hotels had a challenge: to convince the franchisee owners and general managers of its 1,300 hotels to invest in upgrading their properties in order to keep the brand fresh and alive. Gina Valenti, senior director, brand program development and integration, one of the leaders of the initiative, said, "We needed our people to not only agree to make significant investments, but to be excited about doing it. We knew we needed to do something more than get 3,000 people in a room and have our leaders tell them, 'Here's what you have to do and here's why.' To get real buy-in, we decided to use a *Learning Map*® module."

The Hampton team created "Make It Hampton—The Launch" (also shown in color at the center of the book), which clearly showed franchisees the why, what, and how of the initiative. "The process helped reveal the benefits of the changes and allowed people to come to their own conclusions about what such a financial investment could return to them," said Valenti. "At the end of the sessions, people were energized and actually asked when they could start the upgrade! In the end, only one franchisee chose not to make the investments. That's amazing!" The Make It Hampton

Launching an initiative at Hampton Hotels.

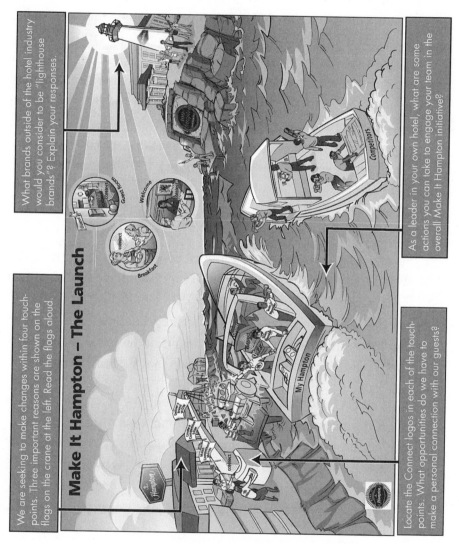

initiative successfully rolled out 127 changes in the remaining hotels in just 12 months.

Hampton leaders found that engagement really adds up. Following the initiative's implementation, they used Gallup's Q^{12} assessment, which includes specific questions that determine employee engagement, to measure progress. Of 100 randomly selected hotels in different markets, 70 responded that their engagement was "good." Hampton leaders then measured engagement of these 70 and learned that, between the 30 that scored highest in engagement and the 30 lowest, there was a 14 percent differential in RevPAR (revenue per available room), and compared with the 30 hotels of the original 100 that *didn't* respond, there was a 20 percent differential in RevPAR.

HONG KONG'S GOAL

Several years ago, Hong Kong pursued a goal: to become "Asia's World City," a destination for business. Government leaders had challenged its public servants to craft "bold and imaginative" reforms to public services while keeping budgets tight. Leaders had many internal and external barriers to launching this initiative. These were some of the obstacles that the leaders faced:

- The certainty that some services would be scrapped and others strengthened to fit new government priorities.
- Increasing competition due to globalization and the emergence of other Asian economies, especially those of Singapore, Taipei, Shanghai, and Sydney.
- An economic downturn that would affect agencies across the board.
- The need to provide excellent service, as demanded by both the citizens of Hong Kong and the public servants themselves.
- The increasing pace of technology and the need to stay current in this field.

- Mismatched skills in the public services workforce, and the need for ongoing training for employees.
- The need to work more closely with the private sector.
- The need to break down walls between departments and work as an integrated team, which required a mind-set change.

To communicate the challenges, opportunities, and changes needed to transform Hong Kong into "Asia's World City" and become the destination city for businesses in Asia, the public service leaders created a *Learning Map*® module entitled "Destination: Asia's World City" (next page, also shown in color at the center of the book).

Over a four-day period, more than 14,000 government employees discussed Hong Kong's competitiveness compared with other Asian and world cities, the government's dedication to quality, and the desire to uphold its traditional values. The public servants engaged in conversations about the characteristics of a world city, competitors and partners, yesterday's world, and the "Typhoon of Change." Here are several of the questions that participants discussed:

- What changes have taken place in Hong Kong over the past 20 years?
- What impact has globalization had on Hong Kong?
- What have you done to respond positively to the forces present in the Typhoon of Change?
- How does Hong Kong compare with other world cities in attracting and retaining customers?
- Which characteristics of a world city has Hong Kong already achieved and which does it need to develop further?

After the sessions, a participant survey showed that 80 percent or more of the attendees had a better understanding of the challenges ahead, recognized that significant change was needed, and

Defining a brand for Hong Kong.

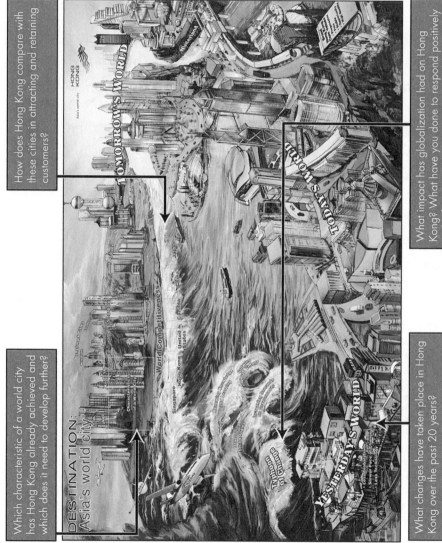

felt positive about implementing the changes necessary to make Hong Kong "Asia's World City." Today, Hong Kong is one of the most active business districts in the world.

THE POWER OF *LEARNING MAP®* MODULES

Learning Map® modules are a powerful means of creating an easy-to-use, common language for all people to understand and get into the game of their business. Maps appeal to the various ways in which people learn and process information. They represent a safe environment in which people can explore and understand what is often ambiguous and unclear. But in the end, like any great map, they allow people from all backgrounds and all levels to understand the common journey that everyone is on and how to help the company arrive at its strategic destination.

QUESTIONS FOR ACTION

1. *What kind of maps have helped you navigate an important journey in your life? How did the map help? What would it have been like without the map? As a result of using the map, how much do you remember about the journey?*

2. *Have you ever used a map of any kind with other people? What was your conversation like? What could you figure out together that you might not have figured out alone? Once you chose your course, what was the level of shared buy-in?*

3. *Where in your business is a component of your strategy or a business system unclear or not effectively translated into ownership and execution with your people? Could the concepts of a* Learning Map® *module help in the translation process? If so, how?*

4. *Without the help of an artist or fancy graphics, consider building a "learning map" on your own using stick figure drawings, critical questions, and a few important charts. How could arranging all these on a table and bringing a small group together for dialogue help people execute the imperatives of your business strategy?*

5. *Why do you think anyone would go through all the effort to orchestrate a* Learning Map® *experience when it's so much easier to just explain the conclusion? Where have you done it either way, and what results did you get?*

15

Key #6: Practicing before Performing

Most businesses are rife with stories of corporate survival, transformative change, or unique and unseized opportunities that are just around the corner. Yet each story has a common and consistent roadblock to the promised land. That roadblock is how to get people to take action in areas that are unfamiliar and that make them uncomfortable. So how do you engage people to take the risks that they've become very good at avoiding? How do you get them to actively engage in the stories of your business by writing the future chapters? It starts with recognizing the reality that most people want to or, even better, *need* to practice in a safe environment before they will enthusiastically engage in actions that put them personally at risk.

Consider the role that practice and failure play in any new undertaking. Success of any kind requires a stream of continued small failures. This concept is at the very foundation of artfully helping people change their behaviors. People can't succeed if they don't fail, and people need a safe *place* to fail. Practice converts failures into better real-life performances. If it seems obvious to say that practice is the best way to

> **People can't succeed if they don't fail, and people need a safe place to fail.**

take performance to a higher level, it's equally obvious that businesses aren't doing enough practicing—especially when deploying strategy. But in business, when you only have one chance to get it right, how do you practice?

FROM FLIGHT SIMULATORS TO BROADWAY

Practicing before you perform is the premise of simulations. Whether they're physical, with a "live" group of people, or computer-based and solitary, simulations represent an attempt to model real-life situations. Simulations are a way to look at whole systems in order to help people see and understand complex chains of cause and effect. By changing variables or behaviors, people can easily perceive the impact of their decisions on the results.

An example: the flight simulator. No pilot is allowed to step into the cockpit of a plane with hundreds of lives at stake without having spent adequate time on a flight simulator. The cast of a Broadway show rehearses for months before opening night, and once the season begins, they continue to practice. In each example, rehearsal and practice—with failure and *the acceptance of failure*—are part of the pre-performance routine.

> **P**ractice converts failures into better real-life performances.

Sometimes in business, we rehearse before we perform. New hires usually go through an orientation. Salespeople learn new skills so that they'll become more productive. The whole company may practice when a new ERP system is implemented. However, we rarely consider the role of practice in engaging people to execute strategy.

Strategies are all about change, and change requires risk—lots of it. Introducing a new strategy or improving the execution of an existing one involves more than good communication. People's roles, responsibilities, skills, and behaviors are all expected to change. When we don't offer a safe way to practice, most people choose not to take the risk. The key is to create safe places where they can practice before they have to perform. The greatest advantage of learning through simulation is that employees can separate real customer experiences and real dollar expenditures from the failure that's necessary to ultimately succeed. The alternative is to "fail on stage," which is expensive, slow, embarrassing, detrimental, and sometimes fatal to a company.

PRACTICING BEFORE PERFORMING ENABLES A SENSE OF BELONGING

Having a safe place in which people can practice before they perform encourages the type of engagement that helps them feel they belong. As we saw in Chapter 3, a sense of belonging is one of the roots of engagement. Requiring people to change destabilizes their sense that they belong, that they fit. These fears become little mental voices that suggest, "I can't make the change," "Somebody else might find out I can't make the change," and "I'm no longer valuable to the company's future plans." Practice converts these fears of exclusion into a sense of belonging by expanding critical thinking, building self-trust and trust in management, and establishing "practice feedback" as a mutual expectation between employees and managers.

Practice builds critical thinking. With practice and simulation, you aren't only teaching facts, you're building critical thinking skills. You're teaching people how to make better decisions. You're providing a framework that allows people to make mistakes. This framework values failure as a crucial step in the development of people's judgment. It establishes that it is safe to constantly analyze the impact of decisions, both good and bad. You're perpetually trying to improve the quality of those decisions by coming to your own conclusions about what works and what doesn't. By establishing practice as a way to expand judgment and decision-making, you combat the fear that there is one big test coming that you won't pass.

Practice builds trust. This trust is built first as confidence when an employee concludes "I can do this!" and then between an employee and a manager who believes and reinforces that they really *can* do it. By practicing what's unfamiliar, people begin to see and trust a process where they can choose a path, get good feedback, learn from mistakes, and then practice again. Practice builds self-trust as well as trust between managers and their people.

Practice redefines "feedback." Not everyone takes feedback well. When people start a new job or a new role, the last thing they want to do is fail. They may believe that feedback means "I didn't do so well." But "practice feedback" changes this thinking. During practice, the employee can try, fail, get some comments and advice, and try again without repercussions. The rhythm of try, try again, and continually improve creates an appetite and hunger for the "failure feedback" that can boost performance by a notch or more.

Expansion of critical thinking, building of self- and manager-trust, and creating practice feedback as a constant expectation all matter in helping people take the risks necessary to change their organization. The big aha here is that when people are guarded about making a mistake, when they're unsure if they can make the necessary changes, and when they view constructive feedback as a sign that they might not have what it takes to make it in the future, they begin to feel that they may not belong or fit in the organization. Then those self-doubting thoughts creep in—"I don't get it," "I can't do it," and "Maybe I shouldn't even be here." These thoughts all drive disassociation and disengagement. They cause employees to be hesitant and not live up to their potential.

THE BLOCKBUSTER SIMULATION EXPERIENCE

We've seen that failure is a definite accelerator and advancer of a person's capability, but it's even more powerful with a partner, whether that's a simulation tool or live manager or coach. For several years, Blockbuster Inc. has been using electronic simulation modules as part of its approach to "practice before you perform." James Webb, director of training and field HR, says, "Whether we're deploying a complex strategy or teaching a simple skill, we offer plenty of opportunity for practice, much of it in the form of simulation with a coach—usually the store manager."

Blockbuster believes that to accelerate change, people need to feel as if they are in a safe environment. "Our training model ensures that people are comfortable with failing as a way to learn and execute our strategies," says Webb. Blockbuster uses four steps with associates at all levels.

1. Prepare—The coach builds trust with the employee, explaining what will happen in the training experience. Not only are mistakes *allowed*, they're actually *encouraged*. Blockbuster leadership has a unique view of failure. Instead of looking to test people on the knowledge that they've acquired, which implies a beginning and an end, they see practice and failure as ongoing stepping-stones to greater performance. They are always in a "beta mode" mind-set.

2. Show and Tell—Using electronic learning (e-learning) or simulation modules, every person gets the same opportunity to practice the best way to execute in the store. They get the message that practice is important by making choices and checking the results of those choices. If the results fall short, they learn from their decisions to try alternatives. Learners are invited to ask questions such as, "Why don't we do it *this* way?" This creates an environment in which employees question things and sometimes find ways to do things better. Critical thinking and challenging are not just supported; they're expected.

    In this step, simulation and real-life coaching are combined, as the coach demonstrates the skill with a real customer while the employee observes. What the learner just saw onscreen in the electronic simulation is now happening live.

Then, the coach and employee discuss how the interaction relates to what they learned in their practice session.

3. Coach Practice—Now, the employee practices with a real customer with the coach nearby. The employee can see how their own decisions or choices are made, and they receive instant feedback. This continues until the employee feels safe and confident, and the coach believes the job is being done correctly alone.

4. Coach Perform—In the final step, assessments, observation, and evaluation are used to continue coaching the individual, who is now "on stage"—alone, but with the support of a coach who observes and provides helpful feedback.

After these four steps, employees are assessed on content knowledge. Coaches talk about choices that created the intended outcome, and the choices that need to be improved. "The opportunities for learning are much higher if you talk about the answers that were wrong in addition to those that were correct," says Webb. "The most important thing simulations convey is that it's okay to make mistakes. People learn just as much—if not more—from mistakes. If you don't allow or encourage failure, it limits what people might learn. More important, it diminishes their spirit of engagement."

Training processes like this one are especially effective because they combine electronic simulation and live customer interaction with the safety net of the coach's support.

PRACTICING AS AN ENTERTAINMENT SPECIALIST

Here's an example taken from the 100-plus electronic simulations that Blockbuster has created to ingrain "safe practice before performance" as a way to engage their people.

Because of fundamental changes in the marketplace, Blockbuster faced hostile competitive pressures from multiple sources. The specific challenge was that employees needed to transform from people who just created a pleasant experience for customers to "entertainment specialists" who drove increased revenue. This new role was intended to provide value-added insights for the customer and to ensure that associates always proactively suggest the perfect entertainment selections to meet customers' needs.

In this particular simulation and practice experience, employees "rehearse" how they greet customers, position certain movies, respond to customer inquiries, and make great entertainment suggestions.

Learners can see from their facial expressions if the customers (called "members") are happy or not. In addition, learners also see the level of customer satisfaction on the "Member Delight Meter," which is tied to the financial benefit to the store. The better they can engage the customer, the higher the probability that they'll meet customer needs, and, as a result, customers will be happier

Seeing the impact of actions starts a cycle of delighting customers.

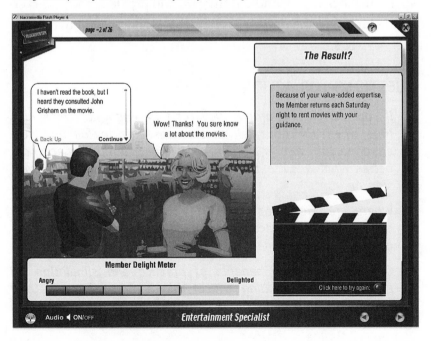

with their choices and have a greater intent to return. This practice, multiplied over tens of thousands of employees at Blockbuster, provided significantly improved returns.

The results are clear to Blockbuster. People who have experienced the modules make recommendations, and they get to "play the game" with a live customer. If the movie the customer wants is unavailable, they suggest another title. They also feel more comfortable promoting complementary food or other product purchases that enhance both the customer experience and Blockbuster profitability.

Blockbuster measures success by assessing service levels in several ways. The four-step model with the electronic simulation has been one of the major components of its improved customer satisfaction levels and achieving lower walkout rates (when people leave without purchasing or renting anything).

Practicing before performing allows people to take the risks necessary to change, to feel as if they belong *exactly at the point* when they began to wonder if they fit, and provides a way to convert failures into the new skills and behaviors necessary to execute their strategy.

QUESTIONS FOR ACTION

1. *If your people are afraid, they can't be engaged. Think of a time when you have felt that it was safe to fail and how engaged you were in learning from that failure in order to get better. What was it in this example that really made an impression on you?*

2. *Where are your people's timidity and tentativeness holding back your performance? How could practice or simulation create greater engagement and results?*

3. *Consider the three benefits of practice and simulation on engagement—expanding critical thinking, building self- and manager-trust, and establishing ongoing practice feedback routines. Which of these would be most helpful to you in*

engaging your people? Would your people agree? How could you ask them?

4. *What performance metrics would improve the most by establishing more opportunities for people to practice before they perform? How could you do it?*

5. *Here are some things you might say to help engage your people in practicing before they perform:*

   • *That didn't quite work—what did you learn?*

   • *Why do you think it didn't work?*

   • *What should you try next?*

   • *How is that different from what you did?*

   • *How might it be better for the customer?*

   • *How can I support your practice?*

6. *Consider the areas where the greatest change of behavior is necessary to execute your strategy. Think of the risks your people need to take to embrace these changes. How could you create a simulator to help them practice before they're asked to perform? You might try asking a sales manager to role-play with a salesperson on the top three customer objections that arise.*

The Process of Strategic Engagement

*I*n Part 1, we talked about the importance of recognizing that human beings work in our organizations. To genuinely engage them in the business, we need to acknowledge and address the things that really resonate with them and make them feel valued.

In Part 2, we laid out the canyons that prevent people from being engaged. These canyons are the major reasons why disengagement is the rule rather than the exception in most of our organizations. We listened to the voices from the field in their own words, through stories and examples. In this way, we identified the reasons why most working people are disconnected rather than engaged in the businesses that they're part of.

In Part 3, "The Six Keys to Engagement," we showed some of the ways that these canyons can be bridged. We outlined proven methods that universally make sense to people, and that are behind the true art of engaging people in an authentic and sustained way. We used stories, images, and voices to explain some tools and techniques that can be used by anyone in any organization to engage people.

And now for something a little different . . .

In Part 4, we'll call on the methods and tools that we described earlier, but Part 4 lays out a process. In any process, there's rigor and discipline. Thus, the voice changes purposely from life experiences and personal stories to the delineation of a process, one that combines all the techniques into a specific method that can be practically applied by leaders in any organization. It's important to see this process holistically, either as a bundled set of activities, or unbundled into individual and targeted actions that can be used to measure the effects of engagement on business results. You'll even find a quick way to measure the current impact of engagement in your own company.

Get ready to take the final steps across those canyons!

16

Strategic Engagement as a Process

As you may recall, in Part 1 we talked about the early days of Root Learning and how we believed that business success would be determined by how well senior leaders could see the future. Our motto was borrowed from Ted Levitt, former editor of the *Harvard Business Review*: "The future belongs to those of us who see the possibilities before they become obvious." We thought we had a winning formula. But then, we experienced the first in a series of ahas. It wasn't the 20-20 vision of senior leaders that would predict success, but that those leaders could create an understanding about the stories of the business—actually more than an understanding, it was an *ability* for employees to think and execute differently in the business. We coined an expression: "Business success will be determined not by the insight and learning speed of the brightest few, but by the understanding and execution speed of the slowest many." The powerful concept of leaders and managers as translators was born. We were driven by the fundamental questions: How can everyone in the organization have a direct line of sight from the "marketplace to me"? How can everyone truly understand the way their business works?

In many ways, we succeeded mightily at this. *Learning Map*® modules and their ability to help people visualize core business systems became a killer application. They were and continue to be used by companies around the world to launch new strategies and execute on strategic priorities. They helped people from Tulsa to Tokyo to understand the adventures and opportunities in their businesses. Even more significant, *Learning Map*® modules changed mind-sets. People genuinely came to conclusions that awakened their understanding of what was going on in their businesses and ignited ideas on how they could help their organizations be successful.

However, there was a big "but." We thought we had the problem solved when everyone could understand their company's strategies. But we came to see that there was an even better way to mobilize all of these methods—stories and images, visualization and dialogue, and simulation and practice. We came to see that merely understanding the business imperatives was not enough to fully engage people and to generate better results. Client after client began to ask questions like "What's next?" "How do we sustain what we started?" "How do we push it further?" "How do we get our people to fully execute a strategy instead of just understanding the business better?" Just as in the days when we thought that astute trend analysis in the hands of a critical few leaders was the predictor of future success, we found that, in addition to understanding, even more was needed.

Our client partners felt that we had a key ingredient to engaging people in strategy execution, but not the *full* solution. Better business acumen made a big difference, but sustained results required more. We started to take a lot of notes on our client organizations, and we became students of the situations in which people were truly executing strategy, and where execution fell short.

To find those missing pieces, we spent the next few years experimenting with various theories and testing conclusions. Then we had our second major aha. In the few organizations where strategy was truly being executed, we found one major difference. Strategic engagement of people was viewed as a *process*, and that process was owned by the senior team. These were breakthrough concepts, at least to us. Until this point, the majority of the organizations we worked with didn't think of engaging people to execute strategy as a process, and consequently, no one owned that process.

We realized that most companies still treated strategic engagement of people as a series of loosely connected events. The roles of leaders, managers, and individuals were not clearly defined. This was most evident when we asked business leaders, "Who owns the strategic engagement of your people?" The

Strategic engagement of people was viewed as a process.

answers were all over the place. Some told us Communications; some said HR. Others said division presidents; some said team leaders. Some simply admitted, "We're not sure." What was very clear was that the vice president of Strategy owned strategy, the vice president of Communications owned communication, the vice president of HR owned many of the people issues, the CFO owned the financial results, and the COO owned operational issues. But no one owned the critical space where all these issues come together and where people are required to think and act differently in a sustained way over time. In frustration, organizations told us that learning wasn't strategic, strategy wasn't understood, and communication was not engaging. But yet, in most companies, no one person or team was responsible for resolving this dilemma.

So we saw the problem more clearly than ever—and saw an opportunity to metaphorically put Humpty Dumpty back together again. We needed to more deeply understand how successful organizations that approach *strategically engaging people as a process* were accomplishing this. We realized that these companies were addressing the different roles of leaders, managers, and individuals, all of whom have unique responsibilities, and wanted to know how all of the interaction among these three groups was being coordinated.

HOW ARE *YOU* DOING?

Before we explore the Strategic Engagement Process in the next three chapters, let's look at a few questions that will set the stage. Answer a simple "yes" or "no" to these 10 questions.

1. Are the people in your organization ready, willing, and able to execute your strategies?
2. Do leaders share a consistent view and interpretation of the organization's strategic direction?
3. Are leaders putting the good of the company ahead of their own areas' priorities?
4. Do the observable behaviors of the leadership team support the strategic direction of the organization?
5. Are managers communicating company strategies in a clear, consistent, and compelling fashion?
6. Are managers reviewing progress with their teams relative to team and company goals?
7. Are managers aligning the efforts of the people in their teams to the company strategy?
8. Does the front line understand the marketplace and organizational strategies?
9. Can the front line clearly connect their individual contributions to overall company goals?
10. Are the skill-building opportunities critical for strategy execution available to frontline employees in their day-to-day work?

If you answered "no" to five or more of these questions, you probably have significant difficulty executing strategy rapidly. You probably haven't managed strategy engagement as a process. If most of your answers are "yes," you have the majority of the key steps in your sights, and your greatest opportunity might be to more consciously connect and manage them as a process.

Many organizations spend little time assessing how well they're executing their strategy through their people. Worse yet, they aren't even thinking about the concept before blindly deploying an onslaught of change initiatives without knowing where they really stand with the current initiatives. This is essentially like an auto mechanic exchanging parts in the hope of fixing your car's problems without looking under the hood, or a doctor starting an operation without first examining you to find out what the symptoms are. We will explore how to systematically assess strategic engagement after we talk about the process.

STRATEGIC ENGAGEMENT AS A PROCESS

As long as there is significant marketplace change, and as long as there are human beings in companies who have ambitions, goals, and opinions, there will be canyons. A canyon is a natural state that exists among leaders, managers, and individuals. Canyons also exist within each of these three groups. The Strategic Engagement Process attempts to create a framework for bridging these canyons and achieving better results.

Whether in major league sports or business, winning is not automatic just because you buy, recruit, or develop great talent. As a matter of fact, more than once we have been involved with executive teams who made us pause and scratch our heads. As we looked around the table, we'd see 8 to 12 people with individual IQs of 160, but possessing a collective IQ of 22. What was missing was not the raw talent, but the ability to find a way to effectively knit that talent together to maximize their contributions. There are many other examples to show that a process can beat a lot of money and a lot of talent—or a lot of IQ. Performance and execution are as much tied to a process as to the phenomenon of gifted talent. A good system beats high talent time after time.

So if that's the case, why do we abandon a process approach in executing business strategy? On the next page, the Strategic Engagement Process is represented in a matrix. The vertical axis shows a familiar way to think about people's general roles in many

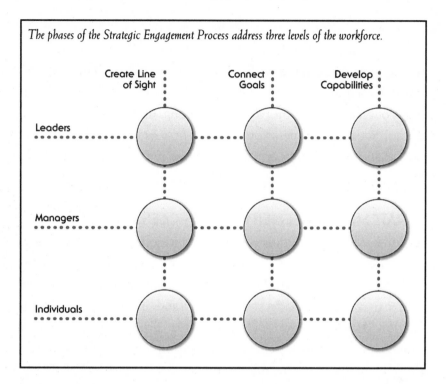

The phases of the Strategic Engagement Process address three levels of the workforce.

organizations—senior leaders, managers, and individuals. It's rather obvious that the perspectives of leaders, managers, and individual contributors in an organization are different. This should be familiar from the Canyon visual we discussed in Chapter 9. The horizontal axis above shows the three core elements of the Strategic Engagement Process. In the chapters ahead, we'll detail how each plays a unique role in making strategic engagement as a process work.

Let's briefly explore the objectives represented in the matrix:

- **CREATE LINE OF SIGHT:** Understanding the strategic plans for the company. This means having a "marketplace to me" comprehension of the core business systems and how they link to the organization's strategy.
- **CONNECT GOALS:** Connecting each person's and each team's goals to overall company goals. These goals measure company

performance on executing its strategy. They also measure team and individual contributions against overall company goals.

- **DEVELOP CAPABILITIES:** Developing the necessary skills and abilities at all levels of a company to execute the company strategy.

While each element can be pursued at different times, there is a sequence or order of attack that is important to consider. First, people need to understand the strategy; second, they need to connect their efforts; and third, they need to develop their skills. The map below, also shown in color at the center of the book, shows metaphorically how these three elements can bridge the canyon.

There's a process for bridging your organization's canyons.

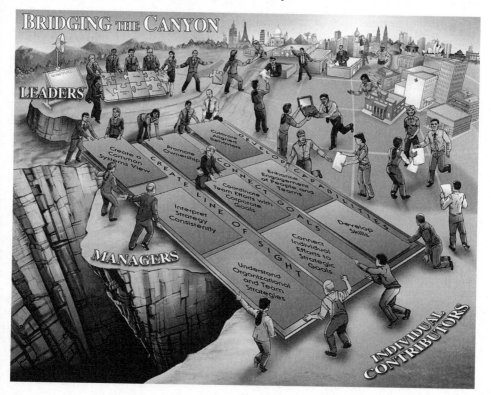

ASSESSING STRATEGIC ENGAGEMENT

If strategic engagement is a process, improving it needs to be approached with the same discipline as any other process—with a solid assessment of the strengths and weaknesses in the process and a clear understanding of how it is performing. This knowledge can open an enormous opportunity for better aligning your resources to the areas with the greatest potential for success.

Engagement is often considered a soft science and, in our earlier days, we underestimated engagement's impact on business outcomes. However, significant progress has been made in the development of methods of measuring engagement. There are now a number of useful tools that help measure how engaged people are in an organization.

Unfortunately, many of these tools only indirectly link engagement to strategic execution. So in essence, they assess how fulfilled people feel at their jobs, whether they have friends at work, and a variety of other factors connected to engagement. What's lacking is a clear link to the behaviors that indicate effective *strategy execution*. If you don't consider the strategic component of engagement, you may be measuring engagement in an incomplete way. In a worst-case scenario, you could have a lot of very happy people who feel "engaged" at work, but they may be doing things that are not part of the strategy that the organization is attempting to execute.

Several years ago, we began working with Dr. Palmer Morrel-Samuels, one of the foremost experts in assessment and measurement design, to help our clients gain insight into their organization's level of strategic engagement. We looked at the observable behaviors that drive engagement relating to strategic execution. We identified 30 behaviors based on research and our experience. These became the core of the Strategic Engagement Process and its nine components. The assessment we developed helps us to diagnose the strengths and weaknesses connected to

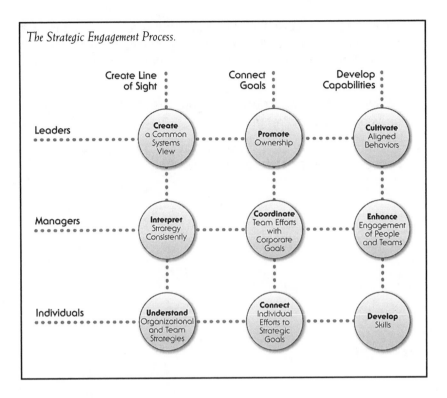

The Strategic Engagement Process.

the process of strategic engagement, defined as "the personal and practical commitment that employees have to the company strategy." All nine areas of the matrix are shown above.

In the following three chapters, we will explore the details of each of these drivers and the 30 behaviors that are at the core of the Strategic Engagement Process.

QUESTIONS FOR ACTION

1. *Do you think of strategic engagement of people as a process? Why or why not? What do you believe is the major difference between approaching strategic engagement of people as a process versus assuming that "great talent will get it done"?*

2. *Where do strategy, communication, learning, and business results come together in your organization? Who manages that point of integration? Does* anyone *manage that point of integration?*

3. *Which of the 10 questions that you answered "no" to earlier in this chapter would be your greatest weaknesses in your attempt to strategically engage your people to create better business results?*

4. *Which of the 10 questions that you answered "yes" to would be your greatest strengths?*

5. *We've shared our ahas and learnings on the best ways to engage people to execute strategy. What are yours?*

17

Creating a
Line of Sight

Let's go back to that cocktail lounge in Chapter 2, at the resort where we thought ideas and insights alone drove business success.

There, we celebrated the end of a senior leader meeting in which we thought we had uncovered brilliant strategic planning ideas that could ensure the future success of the business. You may also remember that the celebration was short-lived, because when we took the best ideas of a few people and tried to get everyone in the organization to accept them and act on them, the plan was an immediate and total failure. The term we used at the time was "dead on arrival." Upon further investigation, it became obvious that huge canyons existed among people and their multiple perceptions of the business. Some people could see aspects of what needed to be done, and others didn't have a clue.

One thing we quickly found out was that people at different levels of an organization fly at different altitudes. They have different views. This is normal and natural, but it doesn't help when you're trying to bring people together to the same level, and engage them in executing a strategy. Consider the metaphor of altitude and what you see from the windows of an airplane. Leaders, managers, and frontline associates fly at different altitudes (photographic representations of these are on the next page), and what they see frames their perspective. Our conclusion was that "altitude matters a lot." Here's what I mean:

35,000 Feet

15,000 Feet

1,000 Feet

The world looks different depending on your altitude.

Leaders fly at 35,000 feet. They see mountain ranges, chains of lakes, rivers curving across the land, and plains and valleys. They see how all these intersect and how one affects another—but they don't see detail, and they don't often know what's happening on the ground.

Managers fly at 15,000 feet. They see cities crowded with skyscrapers, miles of tangled highways, thick forests, and neighborhoods where the houses all look alike. They see some detail, but they are too low to see for miles and too high to see day-to-day details.

Frontline workers fly at 1,000 feet. They see what's on the ground. They see individual cars on the highway; they recognize specific buildings; they see how one street leads into another. They see the water depth in the backyard pools. But they don't see the horizon as the leaders do or how it all connects at mid-level.

A simple question such as "What does our business look like to you?" draws completely different replies from the people at each of these different altitudes. People simply don't see things in the same way. In any organization, to see what's possible, everyone must be able to view the business in the same way even though they're at different altitudes.

FROM THE MARKETPLACE TO ME

One thing is certain: an organization won't adapt and change with the pace, depth, and flexibility necessary to thrive in today's environment unless it first solves the altitude problem. The importance of seeing with the same perspective can't be underestimated. We call seeing with the same perspective having a common "line of sight." Creating a line of sight is a critical component of the ability to engage people throughout any business.

The first imperative for leadership in any organization is to be absolutely clear on the strategy for the business. One of the attributes of clarity is the absence of lies, and we have found three lies that are always present in the executive suite. These are "We have a strategy," "We are aligned on the strategy," and "We have data to support our strategy." These three lies are always in play; the only way they differ from company to company is in their magnitude. The lies exist because most senior teams aren't crystal clear on the strategy. They also stop short of ensuring that they know exactly what the strategy means as it drops from 35,000 feet to 15,000 feet (manager level) and 1,000 feet (individual level). But the real challenge for leadership is finding out how hard it is to make the company strategy clear for everyone else. This is why the creation of a company-wide line of sight is necessary.

A line of sight is all about creating a clear, consistent business language that everyone can understand, think in, and speak. This issue of language is extremely important. Canyons exist between people in most organizations because there is not a common language.

The best way to convey the importance of having a common line of sight language is to explore what it feels like when you don't understand what is being discussed, especially when it personally involves you. Think about what happens when you visit a doctor regarding a medical condition that is new to you. The terms, combination of words, and phrases the doctor uses to describe procedures, outcomes, and prognoses can be completely confusing. As a patient, you can feel helpless—frightened, uncertain, and totally subservient—as you try to squeeze out a small dose of information you can understand. The language of the medical profession can create the feeling that something is happening *to* you rather than *with* you. It's hard to be proactive when you're simply trying to absorb what's being said and translate it into something that makes sense to you. Consider this diagnosis: "The patient has acute pharyngitis with rhinitis." This simply means he has a sore

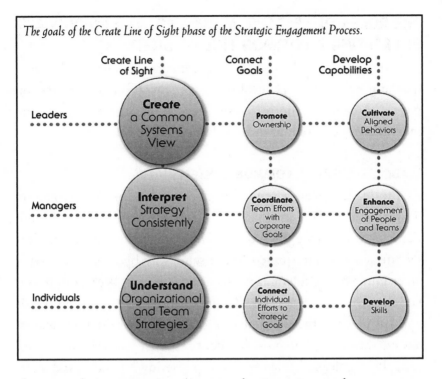

The goals of the Create Line of Sight phase of the Strategic Engagement Process.

throat and a runny nose. As every businessperson knows, most corporate strategies are written in a similar kind of language. They're not really designed for mass consumption. In the absence of a true line of sight language, people feel as if a strategy is something that happens around them, rather than something they're a part of.

A true line of sight is a simplified translation of the business strategy into a language that is relevant to everyone. Without question, the essence of that translation is the conversion of favorite words, common terms, and repeated data stories into something special and unique in an organization. That something special is a shared meaning. *Shared meaning is key*. The most valuable line of sight language is one that creates a common and consistent shared meaning throughout the organization at every level and with every person.

THE ROLES OF LEADERS, MANAGERS, AND INDIVIDUALS IN CREATING A COMMON LINE OF SIGHT

The responsibility for creating a common language of shared meaning exists at every level of the organization. The matrix on page 183 captures the responsibilities of leaders, managers, and individuals. Let's look at those roles more in depth.

LEADERS—CREATE A COMMON SYSTEMS VIEW

At the leader level, a senior team needs to Create a Common Systems View. This involves creating a mental model or picture that means the same thing to everybody in the organization. This picture must be interpreted in the same way by everyone. Here's an example of the dilemma we face at the outset: We've often spoken the word "bear" and asked a group to picture it in their minds and tell us what the word means to them. Our results are almost always the same. The most frequent responses we get are "polar," "grizzly," "Chicago," "naked," "aspirin," "teddy," "panda," and "market." When we suggest that they "go execute *bear*," the point becomes obvious. Words may be familiar, but the meaning is often far from clear; it depends on the context.

Now, try to picture these phrases: "world-class customer service," "growth-based culture," and "excellent value chain." When we read our strategy documents, we all agree that they are priorities, but what is the picture that these words create in our minds? Like the "bear" example, we interpret these words through individual lenses. While unaligned interpretation may be completely unintentional, we can't translate the strategy from paper to action

> **The translation from words to meaning and action is the critical role of senior leadership.**

without a common picture. Words say only so much. The translation from words to meaning and action is difficult, and this is the

One spoken word can evoke many meanings.

critical role of senior leadership. Visualization, as we've discussed in previous chapters, is a very powerful tool for senior leaders to use first for themselves, and then for the entire organization.

It's possible to assess the underlying leader behaviors that relate to creating a common systems view. Here is a simple way to make that assessment. On the chart on the next page, rate the leaders of your oganization on each statement. Award 3 points for a "strong" performance, 1 point for a "passable" performance, and no points for deficiency. We'll explain more at the end of this chapter.

MANAGERS—INTERPRET STRATEGY CONSISTENTLY

Perhaps the most untapped source in the process of creating a common language is managers. Because they are closest to people who work on the front line every day, managers have a tremendous ability to influence the translation of strategy into action.

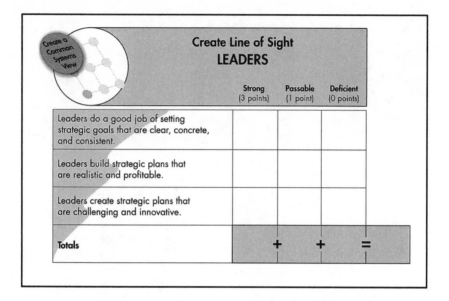

		Strong (3 points)	Passable (1 point)	Deficient (0 points)
Leaders do a good job of setting strategic goals that are clear, concrete, and consistent.				
Leaders build strategic plans that are realistic and profitable.				
Leaders create strategic plans that are challenging and innovative.				
Totals		+	+	=

They are centrally positioned to bridge the canyon between senior leaders' strategic plans and individuals' daily work.

The second enlarged circle in the matrix on page 183 represents the critical role that managers must play to Interpret Strategy Consistently. Often, there are as many different mental models in an organization as there are managers. As all of them interpret what they hear, they filter it through their own experience. Thus, they end up executing wildly variant versions. While leaders must translate the strategy into a language that is relevant to the managers, managers must understand and authentically own the strategy. The question is, "How do they do that?" There are two parts to the answer. First, they must test their understanding of the strategy with the leaders to be sure that their interpretations are accurate and consistent. Then, they must translate the strategy and its meaning in a way that is relevant to the people

> **M**anagers have a tremendous ability to influence the translation of strategy into action.

they manage. This testing of strategy interpretation is a proactive role that senior leaders must invite managers to take, and one that managers must aggressively adopt. Unfortunately, leaders generally assume that managers' interpretations are the same as their own, and managers usually wait to be told that what they're doing isn't consistent with the meaning of the strategy.

Because they must be sure that the mental model they receive is the same mental model that they send, managers hold a pivotal position in creating consistent interpretation of the strategy throughout the organization. This translation is not about trying to tell everybody what they should do, but to help put an understanding of the business into the hands of individuals so that they can come to their own conclusions about what they need to do. In many respects, the secret to success in this task is knowing how to give up control and to listen to what individuals do and do not understand, and then helping them connect to exactly what the strategy is.

Now, to see how well your managers interpret strategy consistently, rate them on specific statements using the chart titled "Create Line of Sight MANAGERS."

INDIVIDUALS—UNDERSTAND ORGANIZATIONAL AND TEAM STRATEGIES

Individuals must rely on leaders to Create a Common Systems View that evokes a universally common mental picture. At the individual level, it's important for each person to understand this common mental model that the organization is pursuing. Individuals receive their mental model from their managers, yet continue to ask, "What do you want me to do?" and "What do you want me to do differently?" When they're waiting to be told what to do and can't see the connections between company strategy and their role, they rarely have personal ownership or change their behaviors. When leaders agree on a Common Systems View

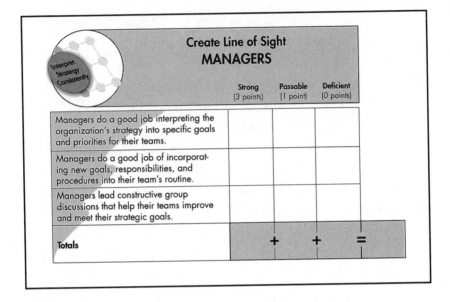

or picture, when managers Interpret Strategy Consistently, and individuals Understand Organizational and Team Strategies, we have completed the first phase in the creation of a successful strategic engagement process. As a result, individuals will know what they need to do and will be really inspired to make the business succeed.

Now, rate the individual contributors on their ability to understand organizational and team strategies. Use the chart titled "Create Line of Sight INDIVIDUALS."

THE BEST METHOD

The best way to create a line-of-sight language that evokes a common mental model is to actually *draw the picture*. Even better than a picture is a metaphor that can capture a business system. In previous chapters, we saw how pictures and metaphors have a unique way of conveying meaning, especially when they're combined with the right questions and dialogue. Visualization has a much higher probability of transporting consistent meaning to all altitudes and levels of an organization.

Create Line of Sight INDIVIDUALS	Strong (3 points)	Passable (1 point)	Deficient (0 points)
Individuals look for and analyze valuable information about our company, our competitors, and trends in our market.			
Individuals communicate with other team members in a manner that's clear, honest, and professional.			
Individuals have the equipment and supplies that they need to get their work done properly.			
Individuals do a good job of planning their work and coordinating schedules so that tasks are completed on time.			
Totals	+	+	=

Note that a line of sight is not the same thing as "a common mental model." The difference is this: a common mental model is what the leaders create in terms of clarity and consistency of the strategy's meaning. A line of sight means replicating that consistency and meaning down through the organization from senior leaders to managers to individuals.

Each of us has a mental picture that represents our conclusions about how our company works and what we are trying to do strategically. These individual pictures drive our actions and behaviors. The challenge is this: We often don't have a chance to compare our own pictures with the external business world, with the actual strategy, or with the pictures in the heads of our colleagues. As a result, we have different versions and no way of knowing which pictures are right and which are wrong.

When we talked about *Learning Map*® modules, we saw that the advantage of visualization as a language is that it can create one systemic picture, a picture that is so simple that people at all levels can understand the business in the same way and "find themselves" at each level. This process is vital to the organization's success. It's profoundly underappreciated as the core of executing strategy.

THE RIGHT CONTENT

Let's consider the content that needs to be put into any organization's line-of-sight language or pictures. Now that we understand the importance of creating the common mental model, the question is "What do people need to understand so that any strategy can be translated into a shared language?"

All businesses have stories. Think of assembling stories in a way that gives everyone a sense of the line of sight from "the marketplace to me" so that people can really understand the fundamental systems and forces. Each business is an organization and, in many respects, it's also an *organism* that advances and retreats, expands and contracts, with a life that can be managed as long as it's understood. The best way to understand the business is to think of it in terms of five building blocks. These include the big picture of the business, the economic system, the customer value proposition, the core processes, and the strategy. These building blocks form the foundation of the content necessary to create a line-of-sight language that everyone can understand. If people understand these areas, they'll more easily answer the five major questions that outline what the business is really all about.

1. *Why change?* This addresses the big picture—the competitive, technological, regulatory, and marketplace forces that are beyond an organization's control but nonetheless shape its strategies. For anyone who's paying attention, they create a sense of perpetual urgency. This big picture is also the part of the business that most people are insulated from, and that explains why new strategies need to be constantly created and re-created.

2. *How do we keep score?* This question concerns the "circulatory system" of any organization—the money flow. This may be a busi-

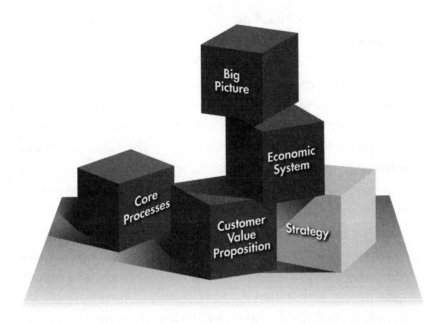

When people understand these building blocks, they'll know what your business is all about.

ness model, a profit-and-loss statement, an activity-based costing process, or the economics of customer segments, to name a few things. They all represent a system that is always changing and must be understood so that everyone knows whether the company is winning or losing.

3. *What do our customers value?* This is a question about focus. It's about innovation and what's relevant to our customers and their lives. Knowing how we segment customers, what their needs are, the solutions that we're providing, and the satisfaction that we're generating is at the heart of the ongoing value of the business.

4. *How do we get it to them?* This is about processes—the supply chain, customer fulfillment, product development, or manufacturing processes. This is where the rubber meets the road. Most major company processes touch everyone in an organization. They ensure that everyone understands how their day-to-day

work connects to the *overall* process that delivers what is promised to customers.

5. *Where are we headed and how do I fit in?* This is the strategy piece that responds to the previous four questions. A strategy by nature is a response to the challenges and opportunities of the marketplace, to the pressures on margin and financial results, to the need for a better solution for customers, and to the need for a more effective way to deliver products and services. The answer to the strategy question provides the direction of a company and how all the pieces connect.

Let's see how this is done in real companies with real pictures and real content. The examples that follow show how organizations around the world have created a line-of-sight language to provide people with a shared understanding of their business and to engage them at the highest level of their thinking.

SCOTIABANK

In the late 1990s, facing new technology demands and changing customer preferences, Scotiabank, a major Canadian financial institution, needed to introduce a comprehensive business strategy that would change service delivery in its more than 1,000 branches. The goal was to develop a customer-focused sales and service culture. This would require a change in everything from job descriptions to Web-based sales management tools, and Scotiabank wanted to transform itself quickly, with a minimum of disruption to service.

To present the strategic changes to employees, the leaders at Scotiabank created a series of three *Learning Map*® modules. The visuals (shown at the center of the book) illustrated a line-of-sight language for the bank. They included the need to change (big picture), the evolution in customer needs (customer value), and a new sales process (strategy). The results were powerful, with more than 90 percent of employee survey respondents agreeing that they understood the strategy, their role in executing the strategy, and the bank's new brand position. The fiscal year following the implementation of the line-of-sight language was, at the time, the most successful one in Scotiabank's long history.

BEAUMONT HOSPITALS

For more than 20 years, Beaumont Hospitals in Michigan were the only game in town in one of the wealthiest counties in the United States. Recently, when two other hospitals entered the market, Beaumont found itself in an entirely new game, one they didn't know how to play. CEO Ken Matzick took 60 days to interview each board member and visit divisions and workplaces. He said, "My sense was that, over a 35-year time frame, Beaumont had become a great organization, but it was very siloed. The focus had been on competing internally, but we needed to come together as one organization to fight external competition. We needed to drive information through the organization to help everyone recognize that the world had changed!

"With significant changes in market forces," Matzick said, "we had to take our story to our 13,000 people. We're a large organization, with significant communication challenges. Yet, there's nothing more powerful than talking to the troops. Employees are key to customer satisfaction. If you have happy employees, patient satisfaction takes care of itself. We needed to communicate a strategy plan that would help us succeed. To engage our people, we created four *Learning Map*® modules to build a common understanding of the challenges and opportunities we faced." (These are shown at the center of the book.)

"We did this by showing how the new competition would impact the business [big picture] and by presenting Beaumont's plan for succeeding in this new environment [strategy]. We didn't stop there. The third map addressed economics—how the business would be funded, the expenses that needed to be paid, and how

Beaumont would invest to ensure a viable future [the economics]. The final map of this series focused on the Beaumont Experience for patients and their families [customer value]. We purposely mixed divisions, departments, and jobs in the discussion groups so that employees would learn about their interdependencies firsthand.

"As we started the process," said Matzick, "people weren't on board. They had their own opinions and beliefs about what we should be doing. Most people leaned back, arms folded, resistant. But at some point, they started to lean in and began exchanging conversations, and even those in very different jobs discovered that they had much in common. They realized that they could effect change. We heard tons of ideas and were told that management's actions to stop to talk to employees showed respect. Everyone felt connected and valued."

Matzick concluded, "I don't think any one person is smart enough to run the company. But together, we all are. This experience highlighted the untapped interest, intelligence, and capability of our people. The dialogue revealed opportunities to refine the strategy, the wisdom to solve our problems, and the involvement to build across-the-board ownership."

After the Learning Map® experience, Beaumont's engagement survey participation rates rose 20 percent, and the organization became positioned to be the leader in a very competitive marketplace.

BEAM GLOBAL SPIRITS & WINE

Several years ago, Beam Global Spirits & Wine acquired assets from Allied Domecq, transforming the company into the fourth-largest premium spirits company in the world. The leaders spent a lot of time integrating the merged assets and the capabilities of the two companies. To get the new organization started in its future direction, leaders found that they needed to flesh out a vision for Beam Global Spirits & Wine before they could create a strategy. Beam leadership started by defining the current reality of the business. They used a water cooler sketch to place the challenges of the business on the table so they could be addressed. This tool was used with the senior leadership team to help drive discussion in an effort to create a clear line of sight for the future direction of the business.

By defining reality, the water cooler exercise set the stage for rolling out the new vision: "Building Brands People *Want* to Talk About." The management team aligned the strategy to deliver this new vision. With the strategy determined, Beam Global leadership created two *Learning Map*® modules to help foster meaningful discussion and build their line of sight: a big-picture map, Tour du Monde, to show the impact of marketplace forces and a strategy map, Beam Global Vision and Strategy that centered on the company's vision (shown at the center of the book).

Following this phase, Beam leaders translated the elements of the strategy into a performance management process with an electronic portal that helped people link their personal objectives to company goals to bring the vision to life.

FIRST LANGUAGE, THEN MEANING

Like a befuddled patient in a doctor's office, it's very difficult to engage in your own life unless you understand the language, can convert that into meaning for *you*, and ultimately see how your actions will affect the outcome. The same is true in engaging people to execute the strategies of a business. The language must mean the same thing to everyone. It must be translated in order to make sense to people where they are, and the content must represent the true building blocks of the business. Equally important, leaders, managers, and individuals must play their roles in creating a language that is interpreted and transferred consistently up and down the organization.

Now, on the scorecard provided, fill in your line-of-sight scores for leaders, managers, and individuals, and total them. See pages 186, 188, and 189 for the scores you recorded.

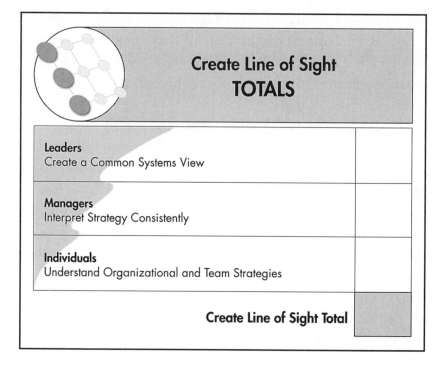

Create Line of Sight TOTALS	
Leaders Create a Common Systems View	
Managers Interpret Strategy Consistently	
Individuals Understand Organizational and Team Strategies	
Create Line of Sight Total	

If your total score is 20 to 30, you're doing well on creating a line of sight. If it's 12 to 19, you're okay, with a lot of room for improvement. If it's less than 12—well, it's impossible to engage people to execute a strategy when they don't understand it.

QUESTIONS FOR ACTION

1. *Think of all the effort you've undertaken to convey to people what needs to be done to execute key strategies or initiatives. What are the roadblocks that keep people from truly understanding what needs to be done and why? What do you believe is really behind these roadblocks?*

2. *Of the five building blocks of a line-of-sight language—the big picture, economics, customer value, process, and strategy—which ones are most critical to helping people understand their roles in executing your strategy?*

3. *If you were to rate your senior leaders in creating a common mental model, your managers in interpreting and translating*

that model, and individuals' ability to interpret and apply the model to their daily work, where is your organization strongest? Where is the greatest opportunity for improvement?

4. *What is your "bear"? Consider the sets of words that describe your current initiatives such as "operational excellence" or "drivers of customer delight." Test them with 12 people to see how many of them perceive the same meaning as you intended. How could you use this insight to improve your ability to engage your people in executing your strategy?*

chapter

18

Connecting Goals

Goal-setting matters. Sometimes we forget the real value of setting goals. For a quick refresher, consider a Harvard study that tracked MBA graduates (reported in *Goals*, a book by Brian Tracy). Of these new graduates, only 3 percent had written goals, 13 percent had goals but they were not written down, and 84 percent had no specific goals at all. After 10 years, the study found, the 13 percent who'd had goals but hadn't written them down were earning twice as much as the graduates who'd had no goals. The 3 percent with written goals were earning 10 times as much as the entire initial group! The only difference among the three groups of graduates was how clear their goals were when they graduated. Goal-setting isn't just important; it's critical to success and can make the difference between a great performance and just getting by.

However, even companies that have developed a discipline for creating goals can lose out on the benefits if the goals are set at different levels of the organization and are not solidly connected. A common approach for many

The only difference among the three groups of graduates was how clear their goals were when they graduated.

organizations is to establish a goal process that combines personal and company development. But many of these processes require goals to be set from an individual, functional, or divisional perspective. These approaches are not intrinsically bad, but they're a far cry from tightly tying an organization's goals to its strategy.

199

WHAT HAPPENS WHEN GOALS AREN'T CONNECTED

Let's use another medical analogy. The human body is an intricate network of multiple systems that must work together to survive. Because human bodies are made up of systems, they are similar in many ways to organizations. As in an organization, whenever a system isn't *treated* as a system, there's a risk of doing as much harm as good. Many health problems result from the inability to reconcile different treatments within one body. Heart medication may negatively impact the liver. A treatment for arthritis may adversely affect the heart. The whole idea is to optimize the connections among the various systems.

By defining what a strategy needs to achieve and connecting its goals across leaders, managers, and individuals, we develop the critical links for success. While most teams aren't dispensing medicine that can adversely affect a vital organ, teams with different goals can have a truly adverse effect on the overall performance of any organization.

The second part of strategic engagement as a process looks at the roles and responsibilities of leaders, managers, and individuals when it comes to connecting goals. This part requires leaders to Promote Ownership, managers to Coordinate Team Efforts with Corporate Goals, and individual contributors to Connect Individual Efforts to Strategic Goals. This part of the Strategic Engagement Process—Connecting Goals—highlights the absolute necessity for these three levels to work in sync. When this connection happens, businesses can bridge the natural canyons that keep well-intentioned people from achieving extraordinary results.

LEADERS—PROMOTE OWNERSHIP

In Chapter 4, we talked about how people can't be engaged if they feel overwhelmed. "Overwhelmed" starts when leaders don't own the whole. This is where complexity and "not simple" are born.

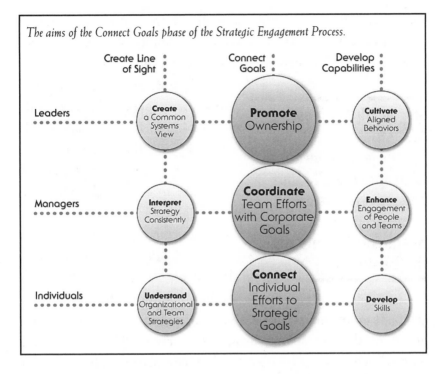

The aims of the Connect Goals phase of the Strategic Engagement Process.

	Create Line of Sight	Connect Goals	Develop Capabilities
Leaders	Create a Common Systems View	Promote Ownership	Cultivate Aligned Behaviors
Managers	Interpret Strategy Consistently	Coordinate Team Efforts with Corporate Goals	Enhance Engagement of People and Teams
Individuals	Understand Organizational and Team Strategies	Connect Individual Efforts to Strategic Goals	Develop Skills

If leaders don't own the whole strategy first, before focusing on their separate priorities, people are often bombarded with each leader's attempt to get the organization's attention and drive their individual agendas. The CFO drives cost reduction, the director of marketing drives brand positioning, the HR leader drives people development, and the COO drives operational excellence. As a result, teams and people are literally forced to make independent choices about what to do and what not to do. This array of initiatives raining down from the top disconnects everybody from doing the same things together.

One of the most important actions for the executive team to take—and as quickly as possible—is to individually and collectively assume ownership of the overarching goals of the business. And yet, I can honestly say that, after working with over 1,000 organizations, we've yet to find a company where this regularly occurs. In literally every organization, it's an uphill battle to get the executive team to put the goals of the entire organization ahead of the goals of their area of responsibility. Virtually all executives agree in concept that their first responsibility is for the overall strategy, but this is rarely how they operate. For example, the CFO, COO, or head of HR landed on that senior team because they represented a special expertise in a particular function, geographical region, or business unit. Exemplary performance in these individual areas is expected. However, leadership dynamics and competition often have most senior team members prioritizing their particular function or unit ahead of the overall organizational strategy. This might have worked when strategies were more compartmentalized, but it won't in a world where markets, technologies, and, consequently, strategies are converging.

> **O**ne of the most important actions for the executive team is to individually and collectively assume ownership of the overarching goals of the business.

The water cooler sketch on the facing page depicts a common dynamic that plays out in most leadership teams. Executives are riding herd on their areas of expertise, and they have little interest in sitting at the table where the overall company goals are prioritized. We've named this approach "goal potluck," after dinners at which everyone brings their own food and places it on the table. We refer to it as a meal, when in fact it's a grazing event that is loosely connected and never organized. In many cases, people who are serious about food politely nibble, and then go out for a *real* dinner afterward.

What really happens here is that the leaders' inability to own the whole first, and be accountable for it, creates an initiative and priority free-for-all. Leaders must consider the prioritization, pace, and sequence of the objectives and initiatives that they put

Leaders must "own the whole" first to avoid a priority free-for-all.

in play. If not, it's a struggle for resources, a struggle for attention, a struggle for sustainment, a struggle not to get worn out, and a struggle to engage people to create the intended results.

Let's look at an example in which this free-for-all happened with the leadership team of a large retailer we worked with. They built a scorecard to run the company, with financial, customer, people, and process metrics. One important metric was manager and associate turnover. Turnover was higher than the industry norm, so the company emphasized the importance of retention. A significant percentage of managers were rewarded based on employee retention. Retention was driven by Human Resources, and this metric became so powerful that it unintentionally became the primary goal for the business.

Ultimately, as managers tried to meet and exceed retention metrics, they kept people who were not best for the business. As a result, other goals started to slide. In simple terms, the wrong people were retained, which harmed the business. Leaders stopped owning what was best for the business and overemphasized just one aspect. This is a great example of a senior team starting with a scorecard that balanced all the key priorities of the business and then letting one metric take over. In effect, they stopped owning and acting on the whole.

Here's another example. In one of the largest technology companies in the world, the leadership team was composed of people who represented numerous "centers of excellence." These extremely bright people developed great initiatives with well-thought-through plans. They had gifted teams ready to execute. When the leadership team was about to finalize the overall direction of the strategy, it quickly became clear that none of them owned the whole. They had spent a great deal of time and resources developing their own piece, oblivious to the whole. Each center of excellence had five to eight initiatives, which meant that the average person in the company would need to work on 25 to 40 significant initiatives over the next 12 months. There was no way that this or any organization could absorb so many initiatives. Those who led each center of excellence heard loud protests from business-line leaders who used words like "dysfunctional," "uncoordinated," and "trying to do too much." But what really happened was that the senior team just owned their own initiatives rather than the whole.

For leaders to own the whole, they must continually prioritize, simplify, and integrate the goals for the entire company. They must also be constantly focused on what people are capable of doing. At times, they may have to sacrifice the areas they represent for the good of the overall strategy. Finally, they must be aware that a senior team who constantly owns the whole is rare. A majority of the time, after the planning process, senior executives go right to their areas of responsibility and pound out their own priorities and goals. In trying to get all these individual priorities and goals executed, the organization often feels as if it is in a constant state of whack-a-mole management. Managers and frontline employees find it impossible to be engaged because they are in a never-ending state of reacting to more requests than they can possibly handle.

Now, assess your leaders as you did in the last chapter, measuring how well they promote ownership.

Promote Ownership — Connect Goals **LEADERS**	Strong (3 points)	Passable (1 point)	Deficient (0 points)
Leaders provide good recognition to employees when we reach corporate goals.			
Leaders do a good job of coordinating strategies and goals at the top level of the company.			
Leaders set clear and sensible priorities for all the units that they control.			
Totals	+	+	=

MANAGERS—COORDINATE TEAM EFFORTS WITH CORPORATE GOALS

Once there is an aligned perspective at the executive level, it's important for managers not just to understand the goals but to effectively coordinate their teams' efforts with the overall priorities so that people and their efforts can be combined to deliver the greatest results.

Effective managers align their team goals with the organizational goals. This is easier said than done. The true art of accomplishing this is adapting and translating critical company goals into the team goals. Managers must routinely talk to their teams about overall company goals and the team goals that support them. By using visuals, scorecards, team dialogue sessions, and metric updates, managers can effectively do this. Teams need to deliver on *managing to outcomes*, not *managing projects*. Projects all too easily become the goal rather than the tool. Let's look at an example.

One of the more prominent credit card issuers in the United States is part of a larger financial institution. The credit card division itself is composed of three distinct groups, each one important to the overall performance of the division. The challenge was to connect the overall goals of the bank with the overall goals of the credit card division *and* each of the three groups within it.

The credit card division's approach began with a line-of-sight effort, supported by three *Learning Map*® modules. The first illustrated the big picture of the credit card marketplace, and the second established how the credit card division contributed to the bank's bottom line. The third focused on the overall corporate strategy and goals.

The major piece in connecting the goals for the credit card division was a set of managers' tools for conducting team meetings. These were designed to firmly establish how the credit card division's strategy and goals set the context for the three distinct groups. Each group had a poster that contained the strategy map and the overall goals of the credit card division. The poster was customized for each team with its own goals included. With the poster and an accompanying guide, a manager could conduct meetings that clearly set out how each team would support the credit card division's strategy. These meetings covered how to brainstorm ideas for action, how to prioritize action items, and how people could set individual goals that would support both the team and the overall credit card division's strategy. The guide also ensured that the same framework and priorities were used throughout the organization. Managers hung the poster in a work

GOALS

- Increase customer base by 25%
- Aim for 100% customer sat
- Offer comprehensive e-transactions

PURPOSE

To offer our customers innovative products and processes that drive real business value

ACTION PLAN

- Expand the advisor role
- Upgrade technology
- Design new products

WHERE WE WANT TO BE

Capability	Measure	2007 Actual	2008 Target	Q1	Q2	Q3	Q4
Attract and retain talented employees	Attrition Rate	43%	35%				
	Diversity	85%	90%				
Create a high-performance culture	Local Business	62%	68%				
	Global Business	72%	83%				
Help customers realize their financial aspirations	New Accounts	12%	15%				
	Closed Accounts	10%	9%				

One way to help people connect team goals to corporate goals.

area so everyone could track progress, and each employee used a journal to replicate the results and track individual plans and achievements.

The credit card division realized some amazing results from this effort. The annual employee survey showed a dramatic and unprecedented increase in the number of people who said they understood how their business aligned to the bank's overall strategy. More than 95 percent of employees agreed that they better understood the core strategy. They felt connected to how the strategy linked to their initiatives, how their behavior impacted the quality of service, and how everyone supported the strategy in daily actions. If the managers had not coordinated the team goals with the corporate strategy, the complexity of aligning all the priorities would surely have caused many people to misinterpret how they could best contribute to the overall organization's direction.

Now, assess how well the managers in your organization are connecting team efforts with corporate goals.

Coordinate Team Efforts with Corporate Goals	Connect Goals **MANAGERS**		
	Strong (3 points)	Passable (1 point)	Deficient (0 points)
Managers have no problems coordinating with other departments in our company.			
Managers create realistic work schedules that impose reasonable time demands.			
Managers give their direct reports the recognition they deserve when they do a superlative job.			
Totals	+	+	=

INDIVIDUALS—CONNECT INDIVIDUAL
EFFORTS TO STRATEGIC GOALS

In Chapter 3, we discussed the roots of engagement: People want to be part of something big; people want to feel a sense of belonging; people want to go on a meaningful journey; and people want to know that their contributions have a significant impact and make a difference. The last one of these is possibly the most important—that people want to know that what they do contributes to the outcome of the business. Realizing that their efforts really matter makes tasks or contributions more than "just a job."

We worked with an automotive parts supplier several years ago. One of the objectives was to educate employees regarding changes in the marketplace and what they might mean for the company. At the end of a set of focus group meetings for line workers, a burly gentleman spoke with great emotion. He said, "I've worked in this business for over 20 years. And for 20 years I have been told how to do my job. This is the first time I've been asked *my opinion* of the business. But even more important, this is the first time that I have felt valued, and I can see how what I do contributes to the lives of the people we serve."

This is profound because it's a *common* experience when front-line people connect their actions and accomplishments to the broader business. Unfortunately, for many reasons, frontline employees don't see how their actions connect to executing the company strategy. As a result, they patiently or impatiently just wait for someone to tell them what to do, or they decide for themselves. In today's fast-paced world, employees need to make decisions on the front line that align with the organizational strategy. Strategy execution relies on their judgment, but when employees can't see the organization's goals, they are often unclear about the decisions they should make and how they should act. If a manager helps frontline people see how to connect their actions to the bigger picture and offers opportunities to prioritize their personal

		Connect Goals **INDIVIDUALS**		
			Strong (3 points)	Passable (1 point)	Deficient (0 points)
Individuals get task assignments that help them meet personal career goals and company goals simultaneously.				
Individuals have work responsibilities that make an important contribution to the company.				
Individuals have input into the strategic decisions that affect their job responsibilities, work methods, and goals.				
Individuals track their accomplishments using objective metrics that help our team hit its goals.				
Totals			+	+	=

goals, their actions are more likely to be in the best interest of achieving the organization's strategic goals.

Finally, assess how well the individual contributors in your organization are connecting individual efforts with strategic goals.

Creating goals that emanate from company strategy requires them to be interlocked and cascaded from senior leaders to managers and individuals in a purposeful way. If goal-setting matters, connecting goals matters even more.

Now, on the scorecard provided, add up your "Connect Goals" scores for leaders, managers, and individuals.

If your total score is 20 to 30, you're doing well on connecting goals. If it's 12 to 19, you're okay, with a lot of room for improvement. If it's less than 12, your proficiency might be stronger in disconnecting goals than in connecting them.

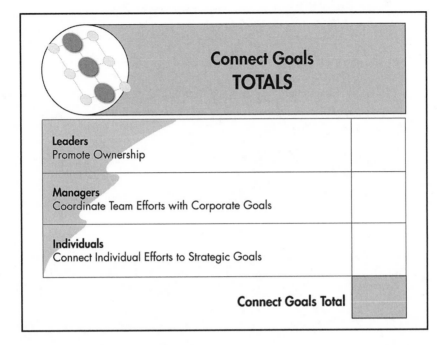

Connect Goals **TOTALS**	
Leaders Promote Ownership	
Managers Coordinate Team Efforts with Corporate Goals	
Individuals Connect Individual Efforts to Strategic Goals	
Connect Goals Total	

QUESTIONS FOR ACTION

1. *On a scale of 1 to 10, how would you rate your senior team in promoting individual ownership of the whole for your company's goals? What could you do to test the validity of your rating?*

2. *How would you quantify the lost resources or unachieved opportunities connected to your responses to question 1?*

3. *In your business, how would you describe the current level of "overwhelmedness"—lack of prioritization, simplification, and integration of company initiatives designed to achieve the organization's overarching goals?*

4. *In your business, what and where are the most prominent gaps between team goals and overall company goals? What could be done to interlock the goals between these two levels in your organization?*

5. *Now, consider only the people you manage. How would they answer these questions: "How does what I do fit into where the company is headed?" and "What do you want me to do differently?"*

chapter

19

Developing Capabilities

Recently, I had an interesting discussion with an HR executive of a Fortune 500 company. He commented that it was the responsibility of his senior team to frequently evaluate their decisions and actions based on the overall growth of their market capitalization. He noted that one of the important influencers of shareholder value is the ubiquitous Wall Street analyst who follows a company and publishes his predictions of how it will perform in the future. As he tracks performances of various companies, he often hangs his Sell, Hold, or Buy signs on the organizations' front doors. The HR executive commented, "I'm getting more and more calls from market analysts like him who want to know about the skills of our people. They tell me that they're not as interested in our strategy 'road show.' They want to know about the level of the skills and abilities of all our people to execute the road show. They push hard to find out what we're doing to close the gaps between our aspirational strategy and our current capabilities to execute it. They're going deeper than ever before to see if we're able to do what we say we're going to do."

This conversation underscored the increasing importance of organizations' ability to demonstrate how they are developing the skills necessary to execute their strategy.

REVISITING HUMPTY DUMPTY

One of our most startling observations over the last several decades is how learning and skill development is often separated from organizational strategy. A company may be doing a great job

of training its people, but the real question is "What is that training supporting?" No matter how high the quality of the training,
it's compromised if it's not directly supporting or enhancing the
skills needed to execute the strategy. It's ultimately the responsibility of people who create the strategy to be involved in developing the skills of those who will execute it.

In most companies, leaders go to executive education seminars,
managers attend training on how to coach people, and individual
employees learn new techniques pertinent to their specific jobs.
But how do these learning experiences connect to an organization's
changing strategy? Where are
leaders, managers, and individuals
acquiring the skills that are specific
to their company's direction?

> **It's ultimately the responsibility of people who create the strategy to be involved in developing the skills of those who will execute it.**

As we've seen in previous chapters, strategic engagement as a
process has three phases—the first
is creating a line of sight, and the
second is connecting goals. The
third phase is developing capabili-
ties. When all three phases are combined, they form the Strategic
Engagement Process. The developing capabilities phase has three
specific drivers: for leaders, Cultivate Aligned Behaviors; for managers, Enhance Engagement of People and Teams; and, for individuals, Develop Skills.

LEADERS—CULTIVATE ALIGNED BEHAVIORS

Building new skills that support the strategy is not just for managers or frontline people. It's crucial for leaders to understand that
any change in strategy requires a change of behaviors at all levels—especially theirs.

We often find ourselves suggesting to a leadership team that
"what you're waiting for will never come." What they're waiting

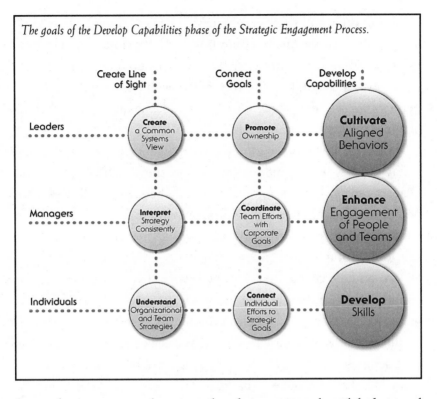

The goals of the Develop Capabilities phase of the Strategic Engagement Process.

for is for everyone else to make the emotional and behavioral changes needed—to go where it's uncomfortable—to execute new strategy. For senior leaders, strategic changes can often be just intellectual. Senior leaders usually start down the strategy road by hiring consultants to help them think through futuristic choices for the business. They wrestle with identifying growth opportunities, isolating shifts in consumer demand, and evaluating the best margin alternatives for the future. This is essential information and key to defining or refining strategy.

> **A**ny change in strategy requires a change of behaviors at all levels.

What's missing is the human component of how to execute the strategy. Senior leaders are often unaware of the importance of changing their and their employees' behaviors. Even worse, they may be slow to personally commit to the behavioral changes necessary to support the strategy. Without this commitment, a strategy won't take root, because the senior team has basically granted permission for everyone else to avoid making the behavior changes necessary to bring it to life.

A leadership team's willingness to align and embrace these new behaviors has a tremendous impact on the speed of execution. Leaders can't just take for granted that old behaviors will work with new strategies. Aligned behavior supporting a strategy acts like a window for the rest of the organization. As managers and individuals look through this window, they can see just how serious leaders are about making their strategy work. Everyone watches for contradictions in their behaviors, and waits to see what the leaders will do. Let's examine a situation that illustrates this.

In the words of Lewis Campbell, chairman of Textron, "It all starts with defining reality." Textron, at the time a $12 billion industrial conglomerate, began a huge turnaround on January 17, 2001. On that day, Campbell initiated a meaningful execution of a new strategy. This was a company whose profits had declined significantly, and top-line growth had stalled. Many financial analysts were questioning the value of a conglomerate business model to diversify risk.

In a now-legendary meeting in Florida, the top 150 leaders were shown Textron's new strategy. In a bold and possibly naïve move, Campbell and his senior team used an automated audience response system so that all attendees could answer several critical questions anonymously. One question was, "Based on this new strategy, would you encourage your friends and relatives to invest in Textron's future?" After all participants had voted, the results were instantly projected on a screen at the front of the hall. Of these top 150 leaders, almost 80 percent said "no."

After this meeting (and after briefly contemplating the painful death of the person who suggested the audience response system),

Campbell sat down to think about the experience, and he had an epiphany. "If the organization is going to change," he thought, "I have to change *first* and, in that regard, I can't be constrained by any friendship, past relationship, or position of a leader."

Faced with the knowledge that the leaders' behaviors were anything but aligned, Campbell arranged a senior team meeting, convinced that he had to personally lead the change he wanted to see in others. He told the senior leaders his intentions in plain language, and emphasized that, in doing this, he wouldn't let any past relationships get in the way.

At that meeting, Campbell used a sketch of Textron's senior leader behaviors as one of the starting points for dealing with the realities that were holding back the potential of the company and its people. The water cooler sketch below that depicted their

When we see reality in a sketch, it's hard to ignore it.

reality showed leaders sitting around a "decision dinner table" wearing masks and not saying what they really thought. They were drinking "nonconfrontational water" and made sure that crucial issues weren't brought up in public. If they really needed to talk about something important, they slid a note into a box behind the CEO's chair reading, "Can we talk in private?" Some of the business unit leaders didn't appear to be as valued as others, and they never made it beyond the figurative "kids' table." They weren't allowed to join in the real conversations about how to operate the business in the future. Several people clearly played by the "old rules," represented by a shield that stated, "I met my number—you can't touch me." The issues to be discussed were on the table, but under a cover that was kept tightly closed. Given that the essence of the new strategy was to become more of a networked enterprise, the behavior that stood out the most was suggested by phrases on the backs of two chairs, where half the group felt they'd be better off together and the other half felt they would be better off apart.

The leaders' first reactions to the visual were, "What an exaggeration!" and "That's not fair!" After a few silent minutes, one brave person said, "You know, these are the behaviors that will prevent us from being successful. They represent exactly why we got a no-confidence vote from our top 150 people." Then, each person was asked to put a check mark next to the one item in the sketch that was most real for them. Twenty check marks later, it was clear that it was *all* very real and relevant to what the team needed to address in aligning their behaviors to lead this strategic change.

One leader said, "We've heard this in other assessments. But when we see it like this, we simply can't ignore the fact that we have to do something about it." Unanimously, the group identified ways to align their behaviors with the transformation strategy of the business and took steps to hold themselves accountable for these new behaviors. For some executives, this was a process of discomfort and personal change. Those who couldn't align their behaviors with the transformation strategy were asked to leave, in a process that was handled with grace and dignity.

At the next meeting of the top 150, Campbell and the senior executives openly shared the water cooler sketch and their approach to recognizing their unaligned behaviors and doing something about it. Three rather remarkable conclusions emerged from the audience of leaders: (1) We can't believe you really know what we're saying about you; (2) We admire your tremendous courage and willingness to be publicly vulnerable in showing us the current behavior sketch and taking accountability for it; and (3) If the senior team is willing to go where it's uncomfortable and align their behaviors with the new strategy, we should begin to do the same.

In 2006, Campbell was featured on the cover of *CEO* magazine, highlighting Textron's successful transformation. By 2007, Textron's stock had climbed from $26 to well over $100 a share. If Campbell and Textron's senior team had never faced reality and aligned their behaviors, this turnaround might not have begun.

Cultivate Aligned Behaviors	Develop Capabilities **LEADERS**		
	Strong (3 points)	Passable (1 point)	Deficient (0 points)
Leaders provide consistent information about performance goals and quality standards.			
Leaders send honest, helpful, and timely strategic information through the organization.			
Leaders have no problems with internal politics, favoritism, and infighting.			
Totals	+	+	=

Once a leadership team develops a common mental model for their strategy, they must determine whether their behaviors match the strategy and are aligned.

Again, assess your leaders using the "Develop Capabilities LEADERS" chart on the previous page.

MANAGERS—ENHANCE ENGAGEMENT OF PEOPLE AND TEAMS

Managers may be the greatest untapped source for increasing the speed of strategy execution in any organization. They are the critical link between converting lofty senior leader aspirations for strategic growth into practical actions on the front line. However, many managers lack confidence, experience, and tools necessary to engage their people on organizational strategy.

Their job is not easy. Managers are in the unenviable position of having to receive and send simultaneously. They must interpret the strategic direction and translate it into real-world activities that are relevant to their employees. Possibly the greatest opportunity for managers to impact strategy execution is their ability to engage their people and teams. But this role is made more difficult by the length of time it can take to make the transition from star employee to effective manager. This calls for reflection on the difference between the master contributor and the masterful engager of contributors. Being a master contributor is all about a single individual; manager engagement is about growing others—making people smarter, more confident, and more capable. It requires changing the mind-set from "How can I beat the competition and become the very best?" to "How can I help my people develop the skills to take their performance on our strategy to the next level?" In an orchestra, the head violinist's job is to become the best violinist possible. But the conductor's job requires getting the best from every single musician. The distinction is critical. Failure to understand this distinction causes many managers to try to conduct the orchestra by furiously playing the violin.

It's hard to conduct an orchestra while you're still playing the violin.

One of the reasons why engaging people is not easy for managers is they simply don't know how to do it. Managers tell us that they are comfortable showing their people how to perform their jobs. They know how to point out where people are falling short and where they need to do better. But off the record, they say, "I don't know what questions to ask my people. I'm not clear about how to respond to the questions they ask *me*. In the end, I'm not sure how to help them figure out what we need to do without just telling them." The skill they need to develop is the ability to engage their teams and people to better execute. Let's see how one company handled this.

When the new leadership at Anchor Blue, a West Coast retail chain, faced a significant challenge for their business, one of their first goals was to create leaders and store managers who would became absolutely stellar at engaging people in the strategy of the organization. The strategy had to deliver significant growth in revenue per square foot and overall store sales to allow the company to perform at a level comparable with the rest of the industry. The plan was to develop managers who could excel at engaging their people to grow store sales. Anchor Blue's approach to building the engagement skills of their leaders and managers focused on four areas: know yourself through rigorous self-assessment, know the business by understanding the big picture, engage peers and teams in the strategy, and sustain the culture.

As part of the effort to build strong leaders and managers who could truly engage teams or individuals, Anchor Blue saw the need to create role models for managers to observe. Then they would discuss the techniques and try to apply some to their own situations. In searching for an effective way to bring familiar examples to the managers so that they could frame their thinking and build their new skills through practice, Anchor Blue settled on a series of movie clips. In small groups, managers watched the clips and then discussed how the interactions in various scenes could be transferred to the workplace. Here are two examples.

Dead Poets Society is the story of a professor, John Keating, played by Robin Williams, who teaches at a conservative prep school for boys. In an unorthodox way, Keating teaches the boys far more than an English curriculum. Through outrageous examples, he inspires them to change their lives. In one scene, Keating stands on a desk to demonstrate the importance of having a "higher view" of the world—a view far different from their perspective as they sat in chairs as students in a traditional classroom. Keating enables the boys to see the big picture of life in the same way that leaders and managers can help people see the big picture of their business. The ability to have managers help the people they lead to "elevate their view" of the business is core to engagement.

In another scene, Keating takes his students to the school's trophy case to consider the idea of *carpe diem* ("seize the day"). By talking about the grand achievements of students who took advantage of their own skills, he encourages the boys to think about the difference they can make in the world. In the same way, retail leaders and managers can find insight in creating the connection between day-to-day activities and extraordinary results.

Keating's charismatic example of engaging his students in their education became an excellent model for managers. These scenes emphasized the idea that this responsibility for connecting contributions and outcomes falls squarely on the shoulders of managers as they work to engage their people in the strategy of the business. Whether it's Keating in *Dead Poets Society* or managers sharpening their skills to engage teams and individuals, these are practical ways in which managers can help others think big and recognize how their contributions make a significant difference.

The second example came from *Remember the Titans*, the story of football coach Herman Boone, played by Denzel Washington, as he worked to overcome racial tensions in a newly integrated high school in Virginia in 1971. During preseason football camp in Pennsylvania, Boone takes the team on an early-morning run that leads them to the battlefield at Gettysburg. Through powerful storytelling, Boone makes a deep impact on his players of both races by recounting how "50,000 men died here, fighting the same fight we're fighting today." Boone stresses that, if the boys wouldn't come together as a team by respecting each other and the game, they would never achieve greatness.

As Boone rallied his players to become champions, managers began to share stories of Anchor Blue team members who excelled at demonstrating the commitments, attitudes, and actions that were vital to their success. Then, inspired by *Remember the Titans*, managers began to share their own stories about their successes and struggles to bring the strategy to life.

Now, assess how well the managers in your organization are enhancing the engagement of people and teams.

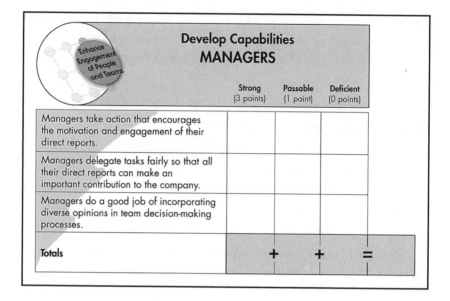

Develop Capabilities MANAGERS	Strong (3 points)	Passable (1 point)	Deficient (0 points)
Managers take action that encourages the motivation and engagement of their direct reports.			
Managers delegate tasks fairly so that all their direct reports can make an important contribution to the company.			
Managers do a good job of incorporating diverse opinions in team decision-making processes.			
Totals	+	+	=

INDIVIDUALS—DEVELOP SKILLS

Once individuals understand the strategy and their role in it, they can begin to apply that knowledge to their daily work. But they must translate this understanding into action in a way that builds their judgment and confidence. They need to develop their skills to execute the strategy. It's here where we most clearly see the disconnect between company strategy and actual skill development. Additionally, as we've highlighted in previous chapters, practice is pivotal.

The sketch on the facing page shows how one organization illustrated the role that practice plays in developing the skills needed to execute the strategy. This sketch depicting several people learning how to ice skate made it clear that these skills would not be developed without a lot of practice, and that falling was to be expected, encouraged, and was part of the skill acquisition process. It also showed that the best way to practice skills was with a manager who was there to convert the falls into new insights for moving the learning process one step closer to a strong performance. In addition, the exact routines that were

Having a safe place to practice and fail makes it easier to feel engaged.

being practiced and mentored were the ones that would help develop the skills necessary to achieve the strategy—because feeling safe and having a safe place to fail are things that every employee needs in order to become engaged.

Here's another example. California-based Panda Restaurant Group has over 900 restaurants and more than 16,000 employees. It's the largest Chinese restaurant organization in the United States. With an aggressive growth plan, Panda faced a major obstacle to achieving its vision—a need for consistent, targeted, strategy-driven skills development. One of Panda's strategic imperatives is to "deliver exceptional Asian dining experiences." Panda wanted a solution that would develop associates' skills and behaviors in order to effectively and consistently distinguish Panda in the eyes of its customers.

Panda created a comprehensive set of 40 skill-development modules that built associates' capabilities in customer service, food preparation, and food safety. These modules blended paper-based educational materials and electronic learning experiences. Panda leadership felt that this skill development was critical in building store growth and achieving its overall strategy.

One example of the way that Panda built skills focused on the Asian dining experience at Panda. Preparing and cooking chow mein exactly as it's intended is an important component of that experience. In one module, the chefs have an opportunity to safely practice combining the right ingredients, at the right temperature, for the right amount of time, with the right techniques. This makes it far easier to replicate the process in the actual kitchen.

When Panda evaluated the impact of the new strategic skill development for the business, the results were outstanding. The stores that focused on this strategic skill development added 2,000

Practicing electronically builds confidence as well as knowledge.

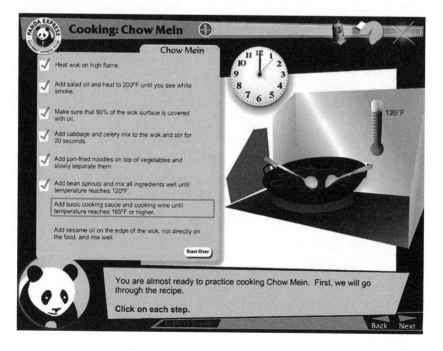

more per-store transactions per year, increased productivity, and improved mystery shopper results.

Now, let's consider a different method. Holiday Inn Express is a franchise company of 1,450 hotels, part of the InterContinental Hotels Group. Skill development had always been geared toward management and had been conducted in a traditional classroom setting. The company wanted to assist franchisees in extending skill development to line-level employees in order to grow revenue.

To create effective and consistent learning, Holiday Inn Express created 30 electronic learning modules in order to enable skill development in several areas, based on identifying and combining best practices in the field. Four of these modules targeted revenue management, a key aspect of the overall strategy. One specific tactic was an interactive electronic game that allowed employees to practice improving revenue—the higher the performance in the game, the greater the skills and abilities to manage revenue growth. Here's how it worked.

The game consisted of a "five-room hotel" where the players were asked to make decisions to grow revenue. The goal was to maximize revenue by considering the variables of hotel demographics, guest type (leisure or business), room rate, length of stay, and period of the week in which the stay occurred. Players could test their knowledge and skill at growing revenue by experimenting with the best ways to blend all these variables. The practice enabled people to understand when higher rates were called for and when lower rates were acceptable—a skill that many employees previously struggled to acquire.

When combined with the full set of e-learning modules, this simple electronic game simulation resulted in a notable increase in daily revenue per available room. It has contributed to increased occupancy. These are two of the hallmarks of successfully operating any hotel.

Develop Capabilities INDIVIDUALS	Strong (3 points)	Passable (1 point)	Deficient (0 points)
Individuals provide effective on-the-job-training for each other as priorities and responsibilities shift.			
Individuals enroll in the formal training they need to build skills that will help the corporation.			
Individuals are offered training that is a good fit with the company's strategic goals.			
Individuals use their skills to complete current projects with consistently high quality.			
Totals	**+**	**+**	**=**

Hannah Kahn, global brand manager for InterContinental Hotels Group, said, "We've seen remarkable improvement in our ability to grow revenue in our hotels by creating opportunities for our associates to practice developing new skills through electronic gaming and simulation. We believe we've locked onto a critical ingredient to execute our strategy."

And now, assess how well the individual contributors in your organization are developing their skills to execute your strategy.

Whether strategies are brand-new or performance on existing strategies needs to move to a higher level, people throughout an organization must be actively building new skills and abilities. In most organizations, there is a real opportunity to better connect the strategy to the ongoing training and skill development efforts in place. The most effective way to do this is to help senior leaders become more skilled in aligning their behaviors to the strategy, to help managers to become more talented in engaging the people

Develop Capabilities
TOTALS

Leaders Cultivate Aligned Behaviors	
Managers Enhance Engagement of People and Teams	
Individuals Develop Skills	
Develop Capabilities Total	

they lead, and to enable individuals to have the chance to practice new skills before they're expected to consistently perform.

Now, on the scorecard provided, fill in your Develop Capabilities scores for leaders, managers, and individuals, and total them.

If your total score is 20 to 30, you're doing well on developing capabilities. If it's 12 to 19, you're okay, with a lot of room for improvement. If it's less than 12—it's impossible to execute strategy and get the results you want if your people don't have the right skills.

So, let's look at the overall ratings that you totaled at the end of the last three chapters. On the scorecard on the next page, simply add your final ratings on Creating a Line of Sight, Connecting Goals, and Developing Capabilities. Then, you'll have a quick idea of where some of your organization's strengths or weaknesses may lie. You can also test whether you and your team have an aligned view of your organization.

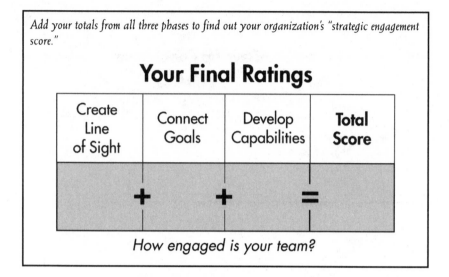

Add your totals from all three phases to find out your organization's "strategic engagement score."

Your Final Ratings

Create Line of Sight	Connect Goals	Develop Capabilities	Total Score
+		+	=

How engaged is your team?

If your overall score is 60 to 90, congratulations! You have a well-connected, engaged group of people who are dedicated, motivated, and passionate about taking your company to the highest levels. If your score is 36–59, the engagement level at your company is passable—but are you satisfied with that? If your score is below 36, you're probably having difficulty executing even the smallest initiatives, and your people are likely feeling very disconnected and unwilling to go on the adventure you'd like to take them on.

Tracking this data over time can help people meaningfully understand, connect to, and deliver on the strategy. It can also be linked to critical business metrics and used as a leading indicator of business success.

Assessing where you stand relative to strategic engagement will allow you to be clearer about how to best allocate your resources. You'll be more grounded in where your organization is making progress—and where you are treading water or may be going under. An assessment such as this enables an organization to truly manage the strategic engagement of its people as a process. And it's a great tool for raising leaders' awareness of their responsibilities in engaging people meaningfully in strategy and assessing how well people are doing their part. Consider it your "people dashboard" for strategy execution. All the efforts discussed in Parts 1, 2, and 3 of this book and the Strategic Engagement Process are wasted if you don't follow up, monitor, and assess.

QUESTIONS FOR ACTION

1. *How aligned are your leader behaviors with your organization's strategy? Which specific behaviors support the strategy and which conflict with it?*

2. *If you were to draw the leader behaviors that are inconsistent with your strategy, what would that sketch look like? What statements would you put in the thought bubbles of the people in the sketch?*

3. *Which senior leader behaviors must be aligned to support the business strategy? How will senior leaders hold themselves accountable to these behaviors?*

4. *How well are your managers developing their skills so that they can translate your strategy to teams and individuals?*

5. *What film clips or other examples could you use to help people see what it looks like when leaders and managers are engaging their people? How could you bring your managers together to connect these film clips or examples to your own business strategy?*

6. *How strongly is your frontline skill training connected to executing your strategy?*

7. *How could you use simulation to create greater opportunities for both managers and individuals to practice before they master new skills?*

Look at the overall rating you've compiled for your organization. Ask members of your team to provide their own ratings, and compare your assessments to see where you are aligned and where you may agree or disagree on the current strengths and weaknesses.

THE STRATEGIC ENGAGEMENT INDEX

For an easy way to get a sense of the level of strategic engagement in your organization, you can use a tool called the Strategic Engagement Index (SEI) to assess where you stand. As you may have recognized, the SEI includes 30 observable behaviors that are incorporated into the nine components of the Strategic Engagement Process.

In Part 4 of this book, we have provided a simplified version of the Strategic Engagement Index. It will allow you to get a snapshot view of where the strengths and weaknesses of your company are relative to strategy execution through your people. When we work with clients on this, we apply a somewhat different type of process, with normative comparisons and analysis of canyons that exist among leaders, managers, and individual contributors. Additionally, we provide comparisons with other demographics within an organization such as department, geography, or location. For more information, visit www.rootsofengagement.com.

20

Conclusion:
Lessons Learned

In working with businesses of all sizes and in dozens of countries, my colleagues and I have discovered some "lessons from the trenches" about engaging people in their organizations. These lessons are embedded in the previous 19 chapters and make up a quick guide for creating new and exciting possibilities for engaging people to create results. The lessons are grouped into three categories: People, Strategy, and Results.

LESSONS ABOUT PEOPLE

1. PEOPLE WON'T CHANGE IF THEY PERCEIVE THE "NEED TO CHANGE" TO BE AN INDICTMENT OF THEIR PAST PERFORMANCE.

In general, nobody likes change. It's uncomfortable. It can force us to take risks that create anxiety. Change can challenge our confidence. When we attempt something we've never done before, we feel exposed, and this sets off our conscious and unconscious defense mechanisms.

None of this is news to even the greenest manager or leader. However, when change is introduced, from the shop floor to the top floor, many people's first thought is, "Did I screw up?" They can easily assume that this change is meant to correct what they should have been doing all along.

Leaders should say to their people, "The need to change is not an indictment of your past performance. What we did in the past worked, but it won't work in the future. *That's* why we need to change!" While this perspective seems like common sense, it's definitely not common practice. But without question, it's the starting gate for successful engagement, and that gate must be lifted by leaders and managers before the race to the future can begin.

2. PEOPLE WILL TOLERATE THE CONCLUSIONS OF THEIR LEADERS, BUT THEY WILL ACT ON THEIR OWN.

The notion that any of us will ever change our conclusions based on *what we are told* simply isn't true. People want to figure things out for themselves. They want to solve their own puzzles.

You can't tell an aha. You have to create the conditions for someone else to make a discovery. Gaining commitments from people—making them believe in your business and want to give it all that they have—requires leaders and managers to set up the right environment for the aha moments. It's an orchestration process, not a presentation process.

For people to change their conclusions, each person must be given the opportunity to think through, compare, contrast, consider, unlearn, or relearn the essential drama and story of the business. In this way, they can discover the drivers, linkages, and levers for future success. When people have a chance to examine all the information and evolving stories of their business, they will come to similar new conclusions. The key is that people must change their own conclusions. Someone else can't do it for them.

3. PEOPLE *WITHOUT* UNDERSTANDING OF A COMPANY'S STRATEGY CAN'T TAKE RESPONSIBILITY FOR CHANGE; PEOPLE *WITH* UNDERSTANDING CAN'T AVOID IT.

I once watched a reporter interview the CEO of a large East Coast financial services firm. The reporter asked why the CEO was spending significant time and money helping his employees understand the company's strategy. "How do you know it's going to be worth it?" the reporter asked. "What measures are you using to prove that you're getting an adequate return on investment for this expense?"

The CEO had an immediate reply. "We spend tens of millions of dollars on advertising and marketing," he said. "Most of the time, we just believe that we *need* to do this. Our competitors are doing it, and we're afraid of what might happen if we were to stop. We're never quite sure exactly what we are getting for our money. But I know this for sure: If we want our people to think about the strategy, we have to give them the whole story. Thinking requires context, and our people can't execute a strategy that they don't understand. And in my experience, once they really understand it, we don't need to ask them to sign silly 'commitment sheets' for accountability. If they really get it, they can't avoid being responsible."

4. PEOPLE DON'T NEED HELP IN STARTING NEW ACTIONS; THEY NEED PERMISSION TO STOP THE OLD ONES.

Few questions are better indicators of timely engagement than "What have you stopped doing in the last two months?" It's really hard to execute a new strategy if you still have one foot firmly planted in past activities that just seem to hang around. We all become creatures of habit and safety. We are slow to let things go, and we hold on to actions just in case they are important.

People need permission to stop activities that they aren't sure they should keep doing. Without explicit permission, they'll generally continue to do things the way they've always done them. But watch what happens when people are given a real opportunity to suggest activities that are redundant, with checkers checking checkers, or tasks that add little value. Most employees will quickly identify areas of ongoing actions that can consume as much as 30 percent of their time. Like pruning a tree or clearing the clutter from your garage, "cleaning up" these behaviors supports the chance for growth. When we accumulate these behaviors in our organizations, we need others to tell us that it's okay to stop doing them.

LESSONS ABOUT STRATEGY

5. STRATEGY IS AN ADVENTURE; EVEN MORE, IT'S A *PURPOSEFUL* ADVENTURE.
Consider the difference in the answers you might get if you asked
a business leader these two questions:

"What is your company's strategy?"

"What is your company's *adventure?*"

If you were asking these questions of a *great* leader, the difference would be startling. Let's face it: strategies, whether stated
verbatim or in some translated form, just aren't very stirring. Even
worse, they're often couched in some jargon that makes them difficult to decipher unless you're in the select group of people who
gave birth to the codes and nicknames. But an adventure? Now,
that's exciting! An engaging leader could tell you a story filled
with drama, and you'd be able to tell from his animated comments
and gestures how passionate he was.

Strategies, if shared correctly, are truly adventures. There are
good guys and bad guys, and the journey is rampant with struggles, setbacks, and barriers. There are accomplishments, disap-
pointments, and refocused dreams—all with consequences that
have real-life impacts on the lives of people. A strategy story, told
properly, is an adventure that invites others to join . . . to be part
of something bigger than themselves, to feel as if they belong, and
to see clearly how everyone's efforts contribute to success.

**6. TO EXECUTE A STRATEGY, PEOPLE NEED AN HONEST ASSESSMENT OF
WHERE THEY ARE AND A CLEAR PICTURE OF WHERE THEY WANT TO GO.**
When an organization has had past success, the need to change
seems less urgent. The truth is, however, that actions of the past
do not guarantee success in the future! Although this lesson
seems obvious, most organizations are less than honest about
where they are, and they aren't particularly clear about where
they're headed.

The two operative words here are "honest" and "clear." Being "honest" requires brutally confronting the facts—about the marketplace, the strategy, the culture, and—maybe hardest of all—leadership behaviors. A leader's first responsibility is to define "reality" in the most wrenchingly honest way possible.

Being "clear" has to do with determining and aligning on what you want your company to create *that does not now exist*—something for which you are willing to endure personal sacrifice, that customers will value, that will provide purpose for employees, and that will reward investors for their confidence. The great value of clarity is that it allows leaders to tightly define what they are going to do together. At that point, they must hold themselves individually and collectively accountable for engaging their people with the same degree of commitment.

7. WHEN LEADERS TRY TO CREATE A PICTURE OF THEIR STRATEGY, THEY DISCOVER THAT IT'S IMPOSSIBLE TO VISUALIZE FUZZ.

Albert Einstein knew about fuzz. He once said, "If you can't explain it simply, you don't understand it well enough." In business, fuzz is the ambiguity and lack of clarity that exist in most strategies that haven't been tested. Sadly, it's fairly prevalent in most organizations.

The concept of clarity is one of the most valuable and least targeted attributes of engagement—clarity on the new direction, the new goals, the new roles, and the new required behaviors. But this rarely exists.

This is where visualization comes in. Visualization creates simplicity. It forces us to think more simply. You can't draw a crisp picture of something that hasn't been thought through in great detail, whether that picture is in your head or on paper. Visualization acts as a mirror for our thinking, revealing just how complete our ideas are . . . or aren't.

If a strategy is not clear enough to visualize, it's not clear enough to deploy or to engage people. This realization becomes obvious when leaders or teams are asked to draw a picture of their strategy and soon find out that they can't, which has led more than one leader to suggest, "I guess we can't deploy our strategy to our people if it's still too fuzzy for *us* to visualize."

8. Good comedians can be more valuable than strategists.

When it comes to connecting individuals to ideas and concepts (as in a strategy) in a way that makes sense to them, great comedians are the real experts. They have a talent for conveying to an audience that they have lived the same experiences, felt the same feelings and frustrations, and reacted in the same way to the ups and downs of life. Simply said, the comedian understands our predicaments. It's this association that makes an audience open their minds, drop their defenses, and offer their willingness to go on a journey together, to follow a story to the end, and then draw the same conclusion.

On the other hand, comedians who aren't relevant—and therefore, aren't funny—and strategists who don't connect to their employees "bomb" when they try to engage people. Strategies, by their very nature, revolve around something that doesn't exist yet. People need to make a leap of faith to commit to any strategy and take the journey. Savvy leaders learn the art of convincing people to make the leap, starting by meeting people where they are and answering their question, "How do I fit in?" Those in charge of implementing strategies could take a few lessons from stand-up comics who know just how to connect to people and engage them in a journey that has meaning, purpose, and fulfillment.

9. People must overcome the "or" and embrace the "and."

As we noted, paradoxes have the power to hold a company back or push it forward. Here's an example of a company facing a paradox. A well-known consumer products company had seven main customer groups, and each of these was valuable to the company in different ways.

The paradox presented to the company's employees was, "What's more important for our future—growing the high-volume customer or growing the high-profit customer?" Some people asserted that without profit, there would be no business, and that the company should decrease the high-volume customers to improve profit. Others argued that without strong market share, the company couldn't maintain its strong industry position, and should do everything possible to grow share, even at the expense of profit. The debate continued until someone suggested that it wasn't really an "or" proposition; it was a paradox that required an "and" solution. Both choices had to be accepted. Ultimately, everyone came to the same realization—the company had to find a way to improve the profitability of the high-volume customers and at the same time find a way to drive the volume of the high-profit customers. This search for continual improvement became the daily focus of the 30,000 employees who were able to understand that the profit-volume paradox wasn't an "or" proposition but one that required an "and" solution.

LESSONS ABOUT RESULTS

10. DIALOGUE IS THE OXYGEN OF CHANGE.

The most effective way to change our organizations and achieve better results is to change our conversations. When we can do that, we set the wheels in motion for executing new strategy. Dialogue is the work unit of changing conversations. As you may recall, *dialogus*, at its very core, enables people to discover or uncover truths by bringing the meaning across. Dialogue expands thinking, and learning requires thinking.

Dialogue reveals unseen barriers, brings hidden reservations into the open, and begins to craft solutions. So, to execute change, people need to execute a change in their conversations— and it must begin with leaders.

Small group dialogue, with people from different backgrounds in an organization, can help people reignite their childlike interest in discovery. When people are allowed to test their assumptions, learn from the experiences of others, and abandon the fear of needing to be exactly right, we unleash a search for ideas that changes mind-sets and individual behaviors. Only dialogue can do this.

11. COMPETITIVENESS IS NOT DETERMINED BY THE LEARNING SPEED OF THE "FASTEST FEW," BUT BY THE LEARNING AND EXECUTION SPEED OF THE "SLOWEST MANY."

This statement may seem obvious, but if you don't appreciate its meaning, it can stop your organization in its tracks. Picture it like this: The senior leaders of a company are climbing a mountain range. The rest of the people in the organization are far below them at base camp. Where is the overall position of the organization? It's not with the leaders—it's back at base camp. What matters is not how far ahead of everybody else the leaders can advance but how fast the leaders can move the entire company forward. When it comes to measuring total performance, the success of the organization is defined by the last group, not the first.

In reality, leaders almost always conceptually outrun their engagement and execution supply lines. Everybody can relate to this. Leaders spend months and months developing a strategy—considering, contemplating, contrasting, and dismissing all the alternatives and possibilities for future success. When they're finally done, they usually craft this into a "strategy-in-a-box" and ship it off to their people. Then the leaders wonder why their employees don't get excited about it immediately. Their employees can't realize how critical the strategy is because they have no idea what went into its creation. The focus must change—the leaders must pull back on assaulting the next peak and work to get everybody to the top of the current one.

12. SUCCESS IS NOT ABOUT A FEW PEOPLE HAVING BETTER ANSWERS; IT'S ABOUT EVERYONE ASKING BETTER QUESTIONS.

There is more drama in business than in any prime-time TV series. The challenge for leaders is how to introduce people to that drama. The continuing saga of ABC's *Lost* draws in people by the sheer number of questions it provokes. All of the stranded plane crash survivors—and all their loyal viewers—ask dozens of questions each week, trying to figure out what's going on and what's going to happen next. So, as leaders, is it better to expose people to the drama by reading them the screenplay, or by asking intriguing questions and inviting their comments?

Success is the result of asking better questions so that we reach deeper insights, which will allow us to more effectively solve the real problems. This continual unfolding of business stories requires leaders to both anticipate and probe for the right questions, the ones that will elicit the next temporary answer—and the next and the next.

A large equipment supply company once asked us to help them communicate the complications caused by industry consolidation and the resulting competition in the distribution channel. As we worked together to help the employees come to the correct conclusions, one of the leaders asked, "What happens if our people don't get the right answer?" I asked back, "What *is* the right answer, and how long will it stay right?" She thought for a moment and said, "I guess it's not about a few of us making sure everybody gets the best answer. It's about all of us asking deeper and better questions about the changing nature of our business and our roles in it."

Maybe the biggest thing we've forgotten in organizations is that *human beings work for us*. The most sophisticated strategy is worthless if humans can't embrace it or be engaged in it. Yet, as we found out with the hot dog story back in Chapter 1, the atmosphere of an organization can be electric, and people can't wait to play if they're really in the game. It's up to all of us to constantly bridge the gaps between people and possibilities by knowing—and practicing—what it takes to tap into the latent, unused potential that's just waiting to be awakened and engaged.

SOURCES

Bossidy, Larry, Ram Charan, and Charles Burck. *Execution: The Discipline of Getting Things Done*. New York: Crown Business, 2002.

Callahan, Tom. "Simply the Best." *Time*, March 18, 1985.

Covey, Stephen M. R., with Rebecca R. Merrill. *The Speed of Trust: The One Thing That Changes Everything*. New York: Free Press, 2006.

Denning, Stephen. *The Leader's Guide to Storytelling: Mastering the Art and Discipline of Business Narrative*. San Francisco: Jossey-Bass, 2005.

Kaplan, Robert S., and David P. Norton. *The Balanced Scorecard: Translating Strategy into Action*. Boston: Harvard Business School Press, 1996.

Norman, Donald. *The Design of Everyday Things*. New York: Basic Books, 2002.

Senge, Peter M. *The Fifth Discipline: The Art and Practice of the Learning Organization*. New York: Doubleday, 2006.

Shapiro, Benson P., V. Kasturi Rangan, and John J. Sviokla. "Staple Yourself to an Order." *Harvard Business Review*, July–August 1992.

Teerlink, Rich, and Lee Ozley. *More Than a Motorcycle: The Leadership Journey at Harley-Davidson*. Boston: Harvard Business School Press, 2000.

Tracy, Brian. *Goals! How to Get Everything You Want—Faster Than You Ever Thought Possible*. San Francisco: Berrett-Koehler, 2003.

Note: For further reading on learning processes, please see *The Power of Learning* by Klas Mellander.

Index

At Root we live by the lessons we have learned through 20 years of experience. Employees are connected to our strategy—and to each other—delivering excellent results for our organization. And for our clients.

Employees want to figure out the issues for themselves.

A picture is worth a thousand "aha!s." Root employees are introduced to a new product using the Canyon Learning Map® module.

If you learn how to bring people together, they will create something bigger than themselves.

Jim Haudan and several Root employees work to build a Habitat for Humanity home in the Toledo area, where Root Learning is headquartered.

Root's Master of Ceremonies and resident comedian is Billy the Bellringer, an Austin Powers-type gent with flashy clothes and fake British accent, played by a Root employee.

Business can learn a great deal about relevance from comedians!

CEOs need to realize that they can't achieve success alone.

Portraits of each Root employee, drawn by Root artists, live on the Root family tree in the lobby of our headquarters.

To recognize their unique characteristics and contributions, employees with eight years of service receive larger updated portraits. We're proud of how many there are.

Our message to CEOs is that if you engage your employees, you will get better results.

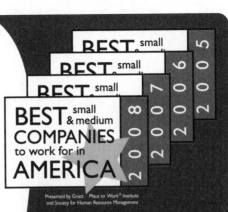

ABOUT THE AUTHOR

Jim Haudan is a different kind of CEO. He has a passion that goes beyond building his own successful company, Root Learning. For the past 20 years, he has been helping organizations and individuals unleash hidden potential by fully engaging them in their work. Jim started his career as a coach and school administrator, and it's not a stretch that the company he cofounded focuses on business learning—the kind that produces real results by engaging people to deliver on strategies.

Headquartered in Northwest Ohio, Root Learning's team, 100 people strong, partners with senior teams at major companies worldwide to build creative ways to execute strategy. They do this through drawing people into their businesses by tapping into basic human curiosity and intelligence. Jim believes that business results don't come from creating a great strategy, but by meaningfully connecting all of the people in the company to bring it to life. And the Root team agrees. The result has been four straight years of making the list of the Best Small and Medium Companies to work for in America.

Jim Haudan leads a group of creative, analytical people who combine art and dialogue in innovative ways. Clients include some of the biggest names in business, including Starbucks, IBM, Dow Chemical, Pepsi, First Energy, Bank of America, and Hilton Hotels—more than 500 companies and tens of millions of people. Haudan wrote *The Art of Engagement* in response to the impact that the Root method has had on such a great number of people. *The Art of Engagement* reflects 20 years of lessons learned in consulting with senior teams at some of the largest companies in the world.

A frequent speaker on leadership alignment, strategy deployment, employee engagement, and accelerated learning, Jim has contributed to numerous business publications. He lives in Sylvania, Ohio, with his wife Michelle. They have three children, Brad, Brooke, and Blake. When he's not traveling the globe visiting clients, he enjoys relaxing with his family at their lake cottage, playing golf, and going to Jimmy Buffett concerts.